Robert Tolf's
South Florida
Restaurants

Robert Tolf's
South Florida
Restaurants

ROBERT TOLF
Sun-Sentinel
Restaurant Critic

BUCHAN PUBLICATIONS

Robert Tolf's
South Florida Restaurants

Published by
Buchan Publications
P.O. Box 7218
St. Petersburg, Florida 33734
(813) 526-9121

Manufactured in the United States of America.

Russell Buchan, Series Editor

Copies of Robert Tolf's South Florida Restaurants can be ordered
from Buchan Publications, P.O. Box 7218, St Petersburg, Florida
33734. To order, send $8.95 per copy plus $2.00 to cover postage
and handling. Florida residents, please add 6 percent sales tax for
each copy.

Contents

Introduction

Welcome to the nation's hot corner of culinary creativity –South Florida, where cross-cultural fusion fare surges into New Wave whitecaps of Floribbean, Flor-Italia, Flor-Asian, Flor-Francaise, Flor-everything and anything that showcases the genius of an exciting group of chefs who merge the harvests of sub-tropical Florida's lands and seas with imports from around the world.

The chefs set the highest standards for grown-to-order produce, selecting only the best of the best seafood, meats, fowl, culling and collating from a tremendous treasure trove of culinary traditions stretching from the islands of the Caribbean to the far reaches of distant continents – Central and South America, Europe, Asia, Africa.

This is your guide to the magic, to the places where great chefs are grabbing the headlines, where the kitchen imagineers, sometimes teetering on the cutting edge of culinary innovation, are joined by passionate practitioners of ethnic exotica.

There's over a hundred different ethnic eating experiences described in these pages which provide escapes and experiences for a full range of palates and pocketbooks, tastes and temperaments, informing those with declining dining-out dollars as well as those with fat expense accounts, from the good ole boys lookin' for a shack where they can get some finger lickin' 'cue, to senior citizens seeking peace and quiet while they watch their budgets.

Tourists, sun-seekers, vacationers, businessmen, dieters, nutritionists and long-term residents can use this guide, a where-to-go, what-to-expect introduction to South Florida's finest, be it in booming Coconut Grove or the world's hottest destination of South Miami Beach, Fort Lauderdale with its Venetian canals, beautiful Boca Raton or Palm Beach with its dash and class.

There are no restaurants in this guide that I would not return to; those who couldn't make the cut, for whatever reason, are not included. I have selected only those places worth the time, trouble and treasure to visit, those which serve knowledgeably selected and honestly prepared fresh food, fairly priced.

Some restaurants of course out-perform others and for that reason we have assigned stars saluting those striving for the summit or already up there:

★   An over-achiever

★★ Front runner in the pack

★★★ Consistently excellent performer

★★★★ Extraordinary performer on all fronts

Robert Toef

How To Use This Guide

The guide is divided in three sections by county with the individual cities listed at the front of each section. Restaurants within each section are listed alphabetically by name, and the index at the back of the book lists each restaurant alphabetically by type of cuisine.

In addition to the individual evaluation, the listing of each restaurant gives the name, type of cuisine, star rating, address, phone number, cost category and meals served.

Specific prices are not listed for obvious reasons, but the following general cost categories are given for full meals for one person, which include appetizer, soup or salad, main course, coffee or tea, and dessert but not including tax, tip, wine or cocktails.

Inexpensive:	under $15
Moderate:	$16 - $30
Expensive:	over $30

We have avoided the use of other symbols such as cute forks or hats, not wishing to force the reader to take a crash course in cryptology; but do advise that you call ahead to confirm current hours, prices and reservations policy.

Finally, an important word about our complete independence in compiling the data for this guide. We work anonymously, sending no trumpeteers on ahead and accepting no favors, freebies, meals or gratuities. We pay our own way and make our own judgments. It's an expensive way to write a restaurant guide but believe me, it's the only way.

EAT WELL AND WISELY!

Miami and Surrounding Cities

This section lists in alphabetical order 99 restaurants in Dade County. Restaurants in the following cities are listed.

Coconut Grove   Miami Beach
Coral Gables   Miami Lakes
Hialeah   North Miami Beach
Little Havana   South Miami Beach
Miami

A FISH CALLED AVALON
Seafood/South Miami Beach

Seafood is the specialty and they handle it with TLC on the grill serving it with some of the best tropical salsas to be found in Florida. Other headliners are the potato-leek soup with caramelized onion cover, crab cakes and the sorbet featuring a bracing combination of pear and ginger.

Avalon Hotel, 700 Ocean Drive. (305) 532-1727. Moderate to expensive. Lunch and dinner. Weekend brunch.

A MANO   ★★
Continental/South Miami Beach

Opened in May 1993 and rambling from hotel lobby to a handsomely appointed dining room, this is a splendid stage for executive chef Richard Chiavari, former sous chef at New York's River Cafe, to flash his skills. We like most his handling of lobster, snapper and yellowtail and the grilled chicken with corn niblets and mashed plantain, served with spinach and wild mushrooms in a thyme spiked corn sauce.The wine list is terrific.

Betsy Ross Hotel, 1440 Ocean Drive. (305) 531-6266. Expensive. Dinner.

ALFREDO THE ORIGINAL OF ROME
Italian/Miami Beach

A long way from the fabled original with the golden spoon Mary Pickford-Douglas Fairbanks lore, but with fantastic roof top panoramas and a kitchen that does more than the famous noodles. There are well-executed fixed price menus and such pleasures as risotto in a cream truffle sauce and veal medallions with truffles.

Doral Ocean Beach Resort, 4833 Collins Avenue. (305) 532-3600. Expensive. Dinner.

AMERICAN BISTRO
American/South Miami Beach

Owned by the same team responsible for A Fish Called Avalon, this indoor-outdoor spread also has reliable seafood. We like the various yogurt combinations, their deft touch with omelets, and the grilled tuna with a mango-scallion sauce. Sensational site for people-watching all day long.

Beacon Hotel, 720 Ocean Drive. (305) 672-7360. Moderate. Breakfast, lunch and dinner.

AYESTARAN
Cuban/Miami

There are many simple, straightforward and casual Cuban cafeterias scattered all over Miami. This is typical of the breed, and a bit better than the rest. Work the line and take whatever appeals. For us that means the roast pork with onions, shredded beef, fried plantains, black beans and rice, concluded with the Cuban custard flan.

709 Southwest 27th Avenue. (305) 649-4982. Inexpensive. Lunch and dinner.

BANG
Continental/South Miami Beach

On South Beach you can start off with a Bang! The name is a logical four-letter followup to the same owners' home base Boom in SoHo. Bang is an art show of figurative frescoes, dimly-lighted abstracts and graphics with cross-cultural cuisine as far-ranging as the huge map mural. Chef-partner Geoffrey Murray—he must have apprenticed in the UN—wanders the world wonderfully with his Japanese seaweed-spinach salad, Balinese stir-fried noodles, Philippine spring rolls, Tahitian tuna, Vietnamese five-spice quail—PLUS Cuban steak, Sicilian snapper, Puerto Rican chicken and Greek souvlaki.

1516 Washington Avenue. (305) 531-2376. Moderate to expensive. Dinner.

BARRIO
Southwest American/South Miami Beach

Breaks out of the usual South of the Border barriers with superb fish soups, vegetarian chili, seared tuna on chayote squash, and cilantro-pesto squid. The margaritas are marvelous and we like the cozy courtyard setting.

1049 Washington Avenue. (305) 532-8585. Inexpensive to moderate. Dinner.

BEE HIVE DINER
American/South Miami Beach

Not a diner by any stretch of the imagination but an indoor-outdoor money-saver with smashing art on the walls, a sheltered patio and a bunch of tables on Lincoln Road for serious people-watching. The salads and sandwiches are fine, the catfish, meat loaf and shrimp served on rice and vegetables are excellent.

630 Lincoln Road. (305) 538-7464. Inexpensive to moderate. Lunch and dinner.

Best Sidewalk Cafe

For SoBe watchers, the News Cafe, 800 Ocean Drive, South Miami Beach, and for Groveites, Cafe Sci Sci, 3042 Grand Avenue, Coconut Grove.

BERNICE'S SOUL FOOD
Soul Food/Coconut Grove

This is the soul-full home of Bernice Cooper who cooks and cooks—chitlins and collard greens, meatloaf and stews, fried chicken and corn bread—-um-um good. The setting and location are perfect, the smiles and sincerity noteworthy.

3547 Grand Avenue. (305) 445-3605. Inexpensive. Breakfast, lunch and dinner.

BIG CITY FISH
Seafood/Coconut Grove

Wander around the $38 million Cocowalk at Florida and Grand Avenue and you might become a believer in the magic of modern developer's dreams. On the second floor, above the multi-screen movies, trendy clothes and all the brightly colored kid stuff that adults buy, is this high tech teaser serving Gulf of Mexico fare— oysters from Mobile Bay and Apalachicola, andouille and Po'Boys from New Orleans, shrimp from Panama City, barbecue from Texas—and fresh fillets of fish from everywhere.

Cocowalk, Florida and Grand Avenue. (305) 445-2489. Moderate. Lunch and dinner.

THE BILTMORE
Continental/Coral Gables

A meal at The Biltmore is alone worth the trip to the Gables. The 275-room, 1926 castle-like monument with its stunning copy of Seville's Giralda tower, its 150 acres, fairy tale fountains, fire-places, chandeliers and out-of-sight ceilings serves you breakfast in the cafe, lunch in the courtyard, snack stuff poolside any time, and formal dinners in El Restaurante where jackets are required. The menu is eclectic and well-executed from the carpaccio starters through the veal and lobster.

1200 Anastasia Avenue. (305) 445-1926. Moderate to expensive. Breakfast, lunch and dinner.

BLACK BEANS ON THE BEACH
Cuban/South Miami Beach

This is the best-dressed Cuban restaurant on South Beach and it's serving all the standbys with class and dash: paella, arroz con pollo with a splash of sherry and roast pork, sliced off a juicy roast with sauteed onions covering the meat, or cut into chunks and then swiftly fried. The black beans are great.

635 Collins Avenue. (305) 531-7111. Moderate. Dinner.

BLUE STAR ★
Continental/South Miami Beach

Star chef here is Kerry Simon, who started his culinary career at a Little Caesars in Chicago when he was 15. More recently he's been learning from the masters at Manhattan's La Cote Basque, Lutece and the Plaza Hotel. In SoBe he concentrates on the high protein, low fat stuff for the calorie-conscious models who have knighted him for his originality and concern for their careers.

Raleigh Hotel, 1775 Collins Avenue. (305) 534-1775. Moderate to expensive. Dinner.

BRASSERIE LE COZE
French/Coconut Grove

Here is the best brasserie in all Florida, the best of all the recent Manhattan transfers, a gift from Maguy and Gilbert Le Coze from New York's Le Bernardin. It's a movie set, an idealization of the quintessential Paris brasserie where Maguy—Guy remains in Manhattan making sure Bernardin's incredibly high standards are maintained—oversees the kitchen which makes what is arguably the best gazpacho in town. And also glorious grilled grouper served on a bed of zucchini treated to basil-perfumed olive oil and crowned with shredded basil, and so much more. It's a beaut, a bonanza, a blessing!

2901 Florida Avenue. (305) 444-9697. Expensive. Lunch and dinner.

Best Diner – Miami Area

The aptly named Gourmet Diner,
13900 Biscayne Boulevard, Miami.

BRICKELL CLUB
Continental/Miami

This 27th-floor penthouse is open to club members only at noon, but at night the peasants with deep pockets can congregate for the panorama view of the new Miami, while munching on salmon-tuna carpaccio, a red romaine Caesar with poached peppers and grilled scallops, followed by phyllo-encased loin of lamb or pan-roasted veal. The wine list is excellent and the service about as pampering as possible without being obsequious.

Capital Bank Building, 1221 Brickell Avenue. (305) 536-9000. Moderate to expensive. Dinner.

CAFE ALLIOLI
Mediterranean/Miami Beach

After the success of Larios on the Beach, Gloria and Emlio Estefan made an additional committment to South Beach in the summer of 1993 buying the 1939 Cardozo Hotel and opening a fine cafe featuring food loyal to its Mediterranean name—allioli is a special kind of mayo spiked with garlic. It's used with discretion by the kitchen which is in charge of a varied regional menu, designer pizzas noon and paella at night, reliably fresh grilled seafood and a variety of pastas.

Cardozo Hotel, 1300 Ocean Drive. (305) 538-0553. Moderate to expensive. Lunch and dinner.

CAFE SCI SCI
Italian/Coconut Grove

This is our favorite Italian ristorante in the Grove. It's a crash course in Italian interior design and culture elaborately laid out in the dining rooms where we feast on Linguine alla Pirata—clams, shrimp, mussels and tomato—saltimbocca or pompano in a caressing pink shrimp sauce. The sidewalk tables are great command posts for people-watching, and feature less formal fare.

3043 Grand Avenue. (305) 446-4863. Expensive. Lunch and dinner.

CAFE TANINO
Italian/Coral Gables

This is another of the easy-to-recommend Italian trattorias that invaded the Gables in the 1980s and thrives on delivering good value for the money. The fixed-price menus include mozzarella caprese, fettuccine with smoked salmon in an Alfredo sauce, choice of pompano, porcini-surrounded chicken breast, or veal chop on a bed of endive and radicchio, plus tiramisu or cheese cake.

2312 Ponce de Leon. (305) 446-1666. Moderate to expensive. Lunch and dinner.

CAFE TU TU TANGO
Continental/Coconut Grove

It's the only second floor sidewalk cafe in the state—you sit along the railing looking out at the pedestrian parade below. The indoor setting is meant to be a Parisian artist's studio—and it is, with artists in residence doing their thing. The menu is all appetizer stuff, the best of which are the Spanish fritatas, beef-chorizo chili, shrimp ceviche, empanadas and that chick pea paste known as hummus.

Cocowalk, Florida and Grand Avenue. (305) 529-2222. Inexpensive to moderate. Lunch and dinner.

CAFFE ABBRACCI
Italian/Coral Gables

The name means "hugs" and owner Nino Pernetti's former Caffe Baci a few doors away—he sold it in mid-1993—calls for "kisses". You'll want to do both when you hug this gem, indulging in the genius of Chef Mauro Bazzanini. His risottos are bellissimo—would you believe a champagne-strawberry christening? His grilled tenderloin medallions in a cremini-barolo-fresh rosemary sauce and waist-wary trio of grilled shrimp, salmon and swordfish with only a drizzle of olive oil and lemon, are major glories of the Gables.

318 Aragon Avenue. (305) 441-0700. Expensive. Lunch and dinner.

CAFFE MILANO
Italian/South Miami Beach

A justly popular open air stunner that could be in mid-town Milan. Check into the great little bar until the table's ready, studying the menu with 11 carpacci, eight salads, a dozen pastas and a pair of risottos. We start with some foccacio and cheese, continue with a light pasta and conclude with a veal cutlet prepared in the true Milanese manner. The wine list is excellent and the service solicitous—if a bit rushed.

850 Ocean Drive. (305) 532-0707. Expensive. Lunch and dinner.

CASA JUANCHO
Spanish/Miami

If you want to impress someone with the cosmopolitanism of Miami, introduce them to this house of John with it's crowds that mass for early evening tapas time. It's bustling and boisterous but it's a great place to watch the fast-talking Cuban community while nibbling on the best selection of appetizers in Miami. Follow that with a full-scale dinner built around a gigantic veal chop, fresh turbot with garlic and Spanish paprika, rabbit cured in Spanish sherry or maybe a suckling pig!

2436 South West 8th Street. (305) 642-2452. Inexpensive to moderate. Lunch and dinner.

CASA ROLANDI
Italian/Coral Gables

Chef-owner Roberto Ruprecht is a native of Switzerland where his Au Fer a Cheval restaurant in Geneva won all kinds of awards. The marvelous manner in which he uses his brick oven here for meats and seafood should bring him new prizes. His breads, desserts and wines are also winners.

1930 Ponce de Leon. (305) 444-2187. Moderate to expensive. Lunch and dinner.

CASANO DE CARLITOS
Argentine/South Miami Beach

The name honors Argentina's famous troubadour, the late Carlos "Carlitos" Gardel. You'll hear his songs while working through the specialties of the pampas. We start with meat and cheese empanadas, then proceed to Parillada Casona, an array of meats, organs and sausages brought to the table for do-it-yourself last minute grilling on a little hibachi. We salute the meats, and Carlos, with some wine from the best Argentine list in the state.

2236 Collins Avenue. (305) 534-7013. Moderate. Lunch and dinner.

CASSIS BISTRO
French/South Miami Beach

Here's a cafe to please the boulevardiers with its careful recreation of something special on the Champs when Chevalier was young. Don't miss the grilled homemade sausages with lentils, the roasted Montrachet goat cheese, codfish gratin with garlic and potatoes and the snapper en paillote with thyme.

764 Washington Avenue. (305) 531-7700. Moderate. Dinner.

CENTURY
American/South Miami Beach

A good budget stretcher with lean, lean cuisine sans red meat but lotsa fish, fowl and fresh veggies. We like the New Age breakast, the pasta with grilled chicken, the clientele from over there—the hotel is owned by Germans and there's usually a room full of countrymen, slim and stylish if they're here for fashion shoots, pink and lobster red if they're simply tourists out for fun in the sun.

140 Ocean Drive. (305) 674-8855. Inexpensive to moderate. Breakfast, lunch and dinner.

CHEF ALLEN'S ★★★★
New American/North Miami Beach

Allen Susser is the creative genius at work here in the largest display kitchen in South Florida, glassed-in and not in full view of all the diners in the understated rooms. He mergers like a magician cross-culinary traditions, inventing a new wave of Florida cuisine that is exciting to experience. His menus are constantly being revised and he organizes all kinds of special dinners; e.g., charred jumbo sea scallop with Beluga caviar and fiddleheads followed by roasted whole yellowtail stuffed with fennel, radicchio and yellow bell peppers; and jerk foie gras with green lentils, smoked tomatoes and crisp plantains followed by fresh water prawns mole with almonds, chayote and mangos; lobster cassoulet with black and white beans, pancetta and seafood sausage. Susser is a superman!

19088 Northeast 29th Avenue. (305) 935-2900. Moderate to expensive. Lunch and dinner.

Best Ice Cream – Miami Area

Nobody freezes it better than the Frieze, 29 Fifth Street, South Miami Beach.

CHEZ PHILIPPE ★
French/North Miami Beach

A highway hugger that presents the pleasures of the provinces with great panache. We like the back room's handling of poached salmon—hold the hollandaise—the rack of lamb, and the whole snapper expertly filleted at the table by one of the experienced crew of professionals. The desserts are worth the calories and the wine list is OK.

13505 Biscayne Boulevard. (305) 945-5807. Expensive. Lunch and dinner.

CHRISTY'S
American/Coral Gables

A steak house of style and substance with gregarious, and omnipresent owner Michael Namour overseeing production of consistently superior prime rib and broiled-to-perfection double lamb chops. But in this brass and wood club setting you can also rely on the fillets of fresh fish and the shrimp scampi, resting secure in the knowledge that few places in South Florida are able to match the baked potatoes and Caesar salads.

3101 Ponce de Leon Boulevard. (305) 446-1400. Expensive. Dinner.

COLONY BISTRO
New American/South Miami Beach

The chef's culinary career ranges from luxury yachts to the Queen of Scots, the Orient Express of the Highlands—coating his chicken with sage before grilling and dressing it up with peppers and prosciutto, and serving fried squid with a mayo dipping sauce that's brought to life with garlic and fennel. Star chef Robin Haas came on board in August 1993 as executive chef and is adding his own Floribbean accents to the menu.

Colony Hotel, 736 Ocean Drive. (305) 673-6776. Expensive. Lunch and dinner.

DARBAR ★
Indian/Coral Gables

This is the premier Indian restaurant in Dade county, filled with memories of the Raj and served by a kitchen in full command of all the spices of the sub-continent and the intricacies of the tandoor. Start your escape with some Mulligatawny soup while munching on samosas, looking forward to one or another of the curries, remembering to order a dish of creamy yogurt raiti if you requested the chefs to turn up the heat. The distinctively orange-colored chicken from the tandoor is also a must, as is Indian beer to calm the fires.

276 Alhambra Circle. (305) 448-9691. Moderate. Lunch and dinner.

DINING GALLERIES
American/Miami Beach

This last remaining altar of Miami Beach Baroque, gracing an important corner of a super-luxe hostelry with all the trimmings, is the best eye-popping setting for the best eye-popping Sunday brunch on the beach. Regular dinners, starting with perfect piroshki and the best lobster bisque in Miami and proceeding through crown roast, salmon in champagne-splashed mustard sauce and something special with lobster, are also events to be taken seriously. The service is surprisingly solicitous for such hotel surroundings.

Fontainebleau Hotel, 4441 Collins Avenue. (305) 538-2000. Expensive. Dinner and Sunday brunch. Jackets required.

DOMENICO'S
Italian/Coral Gables

Caffe Baci alum Domenico Diana, a consummate front man with a loyal legion of fans, launched this spinoff with a kitchen staff skilled in making modern adaptations of the classics. The penne and ziti preparations are favorites of mine, especially when preceded by beef or tuna carpaccio or the Delizie de Mamma featuring artichokes and fava beans. Prime veal is handled with great conscience and the fresh snapper is saluted with a new variation on the old Livornese theme.

2271 Ponce de Leon. (305) 442-2033. Moderate to expensive. Lunch and dinner.

Best Brasserie

The best in all Florida is Brasserie Le Coze, 2901 Florida Avenue, Coconut Grove.

DOMINIQUE'S
French/Miami Beach

This all-suite, all-superluxe hotel is the perfect base for the inviting glassed-in garden space and formally-appointed dining rooms. The modern-day elegance is ever so suitable for the showmanship of Dominique D'Ermo, a French success with a famous restaurant of the same name in Washington D.C. There too the showman sometimes dominates with special promotions, servings of rattlesnake, gator tail, kangaroo, lion and the like; but the less exotic fare, executed by a competent French kitchen, is the real strength here. We stick with the rack of lamb, raised on Dominique's farm and served with caramelized garlic, the chicken breast served on foie gras, and the venison from New Zealand. The Sunday brunch is a happening.

Alexander Hotel, 5225 Collins Avenue. (305) 861-5252. Expensive. Breakfast, lunch and dinner, and Sunday brunch October through May.

EAST COAST FISHERIES
Seafood/Miami

Strategically located in an historic building on the Miami River, once the chief artery in these parts, this fish market-feedery features harvests from the deep laid out on ice a few inches from your fork. That's on the ground floor. Upstairs is a mite fancier and less crowded, but either place you can rely on the freshness without frills. In season we have crab claws. Out of season simply grilled fish with sides of beans and rice.

360 West Flagler Street. (305) 373-5515. Inexpensive to moderate. Lunch and dinner.

EL BODEGON CASTILLA
Spanish/Miami

Not Cuban but classic Spanish complete with a portrait of King Juan Carlos. It is where I take neophytes to learn the finer points of Spanish culinary traditions, and culture—on the weekends there's a full-blown Flamenco show in their upstairs party room. Start your Ole! evening here with the Tapa de la Casa, featuring thinly sliced Serrano ham, Spanish sausage and manchego cheese and then dig into the peerless paella Valenciana with a wealth of chicken and shellfish.

2499 South West 8th Street. (305) 649-0863. Moderate to expensive. Lunch and dinner.

EL MESON CASTELLANO
Cuban/Miami

Less colorful than some others in its league and the clientele constitutes the decor, but the kitchen churns out a reliable parade of solid Cuban favorites from caldo gallego and frijoles negros, white and black bean soups, to fried chicken and pork chunks, steak Milanesa and shredded beef.

2395 North West 7th Street. (305) 642-4097. Moderate. Lunch and dinner.

11TH STREET DINER
American/South Miami Beach

Incredible! A shining silver diner moved to the heart of South Beach from Wilkes-Barre, PA. It's our favorite early breakfast spot—they start serving it at midnight so head here after your night-clubbing. Later in the day come for tuna patty melts, meat loaf and mashed potatoes and other retro comfort foods.

Washington Avenue and 11th Street. (305) 534-6373. Inexpensive. Breakfast, lunch and dinner.

FAIRMONT GARDENS BAR & GRILLE
American/South Miami Beach

This establishment was the winner of a best hotel rehabilitation award a few years ago and they take tender loving care of their quiet and romantically illuminated garden restaurant featuring the kind of food encountered if you sail on one of the cruise ships. The owners supply several of the ships, including the Dolphin and Discovery gliding out of Miami.

Fairmont Hotel, 1000 Collins Avenue. (305) 531-0050. Inexpensive to moderate. Dinner.

FIREHOUSE FOUR
American/Miami

A must stop for frustrated firemen, and a masterful piece of adaptive restoration of Miami's oldest station, vintage 1923. The giant mahogany bar is a marvel and on the second deck you can eat in the space where the officers had their home away from home. Order steak, lamb chops, lime juice-marinated chicken—nothing's burned but remember! don't slide down the pole.

1000 South Miami Avenue. (305) 379-1923. Moderate. Lunch and dinner.

THE FISH MARKET
Seafood/Miami

One of the best seafood servers in the state and certainly the best dressed, this gem is in the heart of a first class hotel, gracing a corner of the lobby where the terrace cafe draws a casual crowd. Its understated marble and mirror setting served by a formal, professional staff gives new meaning to the fish market name. Headliners are the grilled catch of the day, signature soups, Florida lobster tail blessed by truffle-freckled butter, poached salmon in leek sauce, grouper with wild mushrooms. The wine list is excellent

Omni International Hotel, 1601 Biscayne Boulevard. (305)374-4399. Expensive. Dinner.

THE FORGE
Continental/Miami Beach

This landmark has more stained glass than most churches, more original art than most museums and a wine collection that's incredible. The infamy of mob connections and the abiding spirit of Meyer Lansky are also part of Forge lore, and you might have a waiter who reminisces about the "good old days," adding to the legend. We come here for the superlative steaks, roast duckling with a black currant sauce and the fluffy, flavorful souffles, accompanied by judicious pickings from their award wining cellar.

432 Arthur Godfrey Road. (305) 538-8533. Expensive. Dinner.

FOUR ONE ONE
American/South Miami Beach

Rambling through the lobby and courtyard of the 1935 Harrison Hotel with Spanish-influenced Art Deco accents, this 100-seat restaurant has a good selection of designer pizzas and pastas, plus pan-seared crabcakes with almond tartar sauce, lamb shank braised in rioja red wine and steak subjected to the Argentinean chimichurri treatment.

Harrison Hotel, 411 Washington Avenue. (305) 673-5873.
Inexpensive to moderate. Dinner.

GERTRUDE'S
American/South Miami Beach

A one-of-a-kind coffee house cafe with burlap bags of coffee beans on the floor and modern art on the walls—look for the sketch of namesake Gertrude Stein. In addition to the incomparable coffees, there's a tempting array of pastries, good salads, sandwiches and tapas appetizers—and great vibes.

826 Lincoln Road. (305) 538-6929. Inexpensive. Lunch and
dinner.

GIACOSA
Italian/Coral Gables

Chef Alfredo Alvarez is behind the burners and that's reason enough to consider this as a major stopover. His gravlaks laced with fennel and the roasted onion filled with shrimp are suitable sensational starters, but we always have trouble deciding on the main courses after we settle into something farinaceous such as risotto with asparagus tips or porcini, or the papardelle with a superlative pesto sauce.It's not easy to decide among such entrees as veal medallions with wild mushrooms, roast rack of lamb with essence of truffles and fresh salmon blessed with a flattering herb sauce.

394 Giralda Avenue. (305) 445-5858. Moderate. Lunch and dinner.

GOURMET DINER
Continental/North Miami Beach

You can't miss this rugged roadside retreat; just look for Jags, BMWs and Caddies parked in the dirt off the highway, and be prepared to wait. There's' always a line noon and night, stacked up in anticipation of the wonderful salads and sandwiches, seafood combinations, omelets and absurdly tempting desserts. Gourmet is an over-used and much abused word these days but here it's a perfect fit.

13900 Biscayne Boulevard. (305) 947-2255. Inexpensive to moderate. Breakfast, lunch and dinner.

GRAND CAFE   ★★★
American/Miami

Ideal name for this eye-pleaser on the second floor of one of the great hotels of the world, Sole U.S. representative of the prestigious Italian C.I.G.A. collection. The menu is changed daily and count yourself lucky if it includes chayote jimaca slaw, she-crab soup, blue marlin marinated in tamarind-rum and served with coconut-red chili sauce and macadamia-crab fritters. The service is formal and, for the most part, flawless and the wine list is extraordinary. For private gatherings of grape-nuts and friends, the wine room is perfect.

Grand Bay Hotel, 2669 South Bayshore Drive. (305) 858-9600. Expensive. Lunch and dinner.

GREENWICH VILLAGE
American/Miami

This eatery will not remind you of its New York namesake but it will give you an outdoor greenhouse escape from all the high tech highways and overpasses roaring by. The salads are special at noontime, steaks and chicken at night and at any time there are the delights of a fine dessert table.

1001 South Miami Avenue, 372-1716. Inexpensive to moderate. Lunch and dinner.

HARPOON MICKEY'S
American/South Miami Beach

Action center of SoBe for the greet-and-meet single set stacked up at the stand up bars facing sidewalk promenanders. Tables spread out in the wide courtyard are filled with everything from chicken burgers to Maine lobsters, reubens to Caribbean curried shrimp. The clam chowder is worth writing Boston about and in football season the fish of the day is dolphin. When the baseballers are in town, it's marlin.

Clevelander Hotel, 1020 Ocean Drive. (305) 531-3485. Inexpensive to moderate. Lunch and dinner.

I PAPARAZZI
Italian/South Miami Beach

Another of the beachfront cafes that's in a prime position for people-watching, with a great bar and designer pizzas from a wood-burning brick oven. We usually start with the fried squid fra diavolo or a half portion of pasta, and proceed to a snapper flattened with a porcini-flecked marsala sauce.

Breakwater Hotel, 940 Ocean Drive. (305) 531-3500. Moderate. Dinner.

I TRE MERLI
Italian/South Miami Beach

The ravens, the Merli, from Genoa and SoHo nested here with their wine warehouse approach to restaurant design and their highly imaginative approach to northern Italian classic cuisine accented with the best pesto this side of Liguria. If Columbus could have had their porcini polenta, gorgonzola gnocchi and veal-stuffed ravioli, he might not have left his native Genoa.

1437 Washington Avenue. (305) 672-6702. Expensive. Dinner.

IL TULIPANO
Italian/Miami

Filippo Il Grande lives up to his name in this formally-served little charmer, with superior wine list and such specialties as Orecchiette Toscani, ear-shaped pasta with Tuscan beans, swordfish with pink peppercorns, veal cutlet with arugula and radicchio, salmon, snapper and yellowtail treated to sauces from the delicate northern Italian repertoire.

11052 Biscayne Boulevard. (305) 893-4811. Moderate to expensive. Dinner.

JANJO'S ★★
New American/Coconut Grove

The name stands for chef-owner Jan Jorgensen who brought to the Grove fresh breezes from California and the Caribbean; to wit, warm lobster and lo-mein noodle salad with scallions and tomatoes in coconut milk; raw Thai beef salad with baby romaine and lots of garlic; wood oven-fired pizzas; apple-cardamon glazed roast chicken breast and braised lamb shank with lemon-baked white beans and green beans wrapped in grilled pancetta. For dessert you must try the wild blackberry Napoleon and sample the platter of home-baked cookies—I dare you to have only one chocolate rock.

3131 Commodore Plaza. (305) 448-2191. Moderate. Lunch and dinner.

JOE'S STONE CRAB ★
Seafood/South Miami Beach

This is the most famous restaurant in South Florida and it's still specializing in the claws of stone crab, one of the state's great natural resources, but this soon-to-be octogenarian landmark also does excellent fried oysters, cottage fries, creamed spinach, key lime pie. To avoid the inevitable wait, go early for dinner or lunch or use the take-out window on the side of the building.

227 Biscayne Street. (305) 673-0365. Moderate to expensive. Lunch and dinner. No reservations. Closed May 15 through October 15.

Best Old Timer – Miami Area

Who else but the venerable Joe's Stone Crab, 227 Biscayne Street, South Miami Beach.

LA BUSSOLA ★★★
Italian/Coral Gables

One of the most successful Flo-Italia feeders in South Florida, this stunner was opened in 1984 by chef Claudio Giordano and his Peruvian-born CPA wife, Elizabeth. Two remodelings and expansions later, they're in their prime, performing in a Renaissance room of brick, marble, columns and colonnades. Start with some thinly-sliced prosciutto from Parma or roasted peppers with walnut-crusted goat cheese followed by pumpkin ravioli with parmesan and asparagus tips in a light pink cream sauce, grilled veal chop with mushroom polenta or grilled dolphin on a red bell pepper coulis. Finish with some zuppa inglese or it's replacement in the Italian-American repertoire, tiramisu. The wine list measures up to the high, high standards set by front and back room.

270 Giralda Avenue, (305) 445-8783. Moderate to expensive. Lunch and dinner.

LA CARRETA
Cuban/Miami

Simple cafe on Calle Ocho, the main artery running through the heart of Little Havana, and a reliable stop for all the classics of the Cuban kitchen—the lechon asado, roast pork, is muy bueno and we like the casualness of it all.

3632 South West 8th Street. (305) 444-7501. Inexpensive. Lunch and dinner.

LA ESQUINA DE TEJAS
Cuban/Hialeah

This corner of Texas is known as the Pentagon because it's where the power brokers meet and eat, as President Reagan did when he lunched here and caused quite a stir from one end of Miami to the other. Try to figure out who's who as you munch on your boliche braced by a doll house cup of Cafe Cubano.

101 South West 12th Avenue. (305) 545-5341. Inexpensive. Lunch and dinner.

LA PALOMA ★★★
Continental/North Miami

One of the great success stories in the state, this superblymanaged stunner started as a simple little downtown eatery with a few tables and two-person staff, Maria and Werner Staub, Swiss emigres with a great deal of charm, capability and desire to succeed. That was in 1977. Today their restaurant seats 400—very comfortably in ultra-elegant surroundings with lots of formal, pampering service, and accents of brocade, lace, velvets, collector's china and crystal. Seasonal concerts—opera, classical, Broadway— were inaugurated in 1993, with resounding success. The omnipresent Maria is enough of a show for us as we watch her professionalism and perfectionism in action, while smiling our way through smoked brook trout with horseradish sauce, Norwegian salmon hollandaise on spinach, lobster bisque, cheese-filled angnolotti, building up to the entrees of Dover sole almondine, crisp duckling in a blueberry salute, veal chop with morels, or a grilled paillard of chicken—when I'm counting calories.

10999 Biscayne Boulevard. (305) 891-0505. Expensive. Dinner.

LARIOS ON THE BEACH
Cuban/South Miami Beach

This was Gloria and husband Emilio Estefan's initial investment on SoBe and they brought in their favorite Cuban neighborhood restaurateurs, the Larios, to run it. Lunch or munch some pickled kingfish or one of those lusciously layered Cuban sandwiches. At night we like the boiled ham hock, the Lacon con Papas, pot roast, or shrimp swimming in garlic, Camarones al Ajillo, followed by flan of course—it comes plain, with cheese, pineapple or coffee flavors.

820 Ocean Drive. (305) 532-9577. Inexpensive to moderate. Breakfast, lunch and dinner.

LAS PUERTAS
Mexican/Coral Gables

Calls itself the House of the Chile Pepper, but it's oh so much more with its marinated shrimp-scallop combination, pork slow-cooked in banana leaves with orange juice, then rolled in tortillas and served with red onion salsa; roast poblano stuffed with cheese, fried and crowned with Mexican chorizo; and corn tortilla-crusted yellowtail served with black beans, and an orange tomatillo salsa.

148 Giralda Avenue. (305) 442-0708. Inexpensive. Lunch and dinner.

LAS TAPAS
Spanish/Miami

For a quick trip to Spain head for this wonderful recreation of tapas bars in Madrid, one with a grand variety of those saucer-filling appetizers. Sure all those sausages and hams hanging overhead are plastic, but they form a fun frame for the on-view grill chefs preparing your langoustine, shrimp, chicken and steak in the Spanish—not Cuban—manner. Be sure to have a bowl of the classic white bean soup, caldo gallego, for a starter.

Bayside Marketplace, 401 Biscayne Boulevard. (305) 372-2737. Inexpensive to moderate. Lunch and dinner.

THE LAZY LIZARD
Southwest American/South Miami Beach

Funky Tex-Mex kind of place with indoor-outdoor seating and such routine-smashing specialties as breast of chicken with their own chile mole sauce, pork roast glazed with hot apple jelly, duck fajitas and little pizzas sprinkled with Mexican oregano, Monterey Jack and goat cheeses.

646 Lincoln Road. (305) 532-2809. Inexpensive. Lunch and dinner.

LE FESTIVAL ★★★★
French/Coral Gables

Since 1974 this elegantly appointed and served French enclave has rested comfortably on the summit and today, under the ownership and direction of Ramon Rodriguez, who took over in 1992 but kept the veteran staff, it's as good as ever. Order anything with salmon, the red snapper with a champagne-kissed basil sauce, a veal chop crowned with rosemary twigs and thyme, grilled tournedos saluted with bearnaise, or Le Poulet Chateau Chambord, a breast of baby chicken treated royally to chestnut puree and raspberry sauce sporting a sprinkle of whole berries. The dessert cart is a real stunner.

2120 Salzedo Street. (305) 442-8545. Expensive. Lunch and dinner.

LE PAVILLON ★★
Continental/Miami

The best bet for Le Grand Affaire, on the lobby level of a 31-story stunner, past the knock-out Henry Moore sculpture surrounded with marble and woods from half the quarries and forests of the world. The room is super sophisticated, the service flawless, the wine list extensive, the cheffing sensational without getting over cute or Nouvelle Miami. The Sunday brunch is to die for. The only drawback is the lack of a view of beautiful Biscayne Bay and the Cruise Port.

Intercontinental Hotel, 100 Chopin Plaza, Biscayne Boulevard. (305) 577-1000. Moderate to expensive. Lunch and dinner.

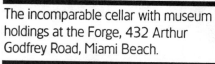

Best Wine List – Miami Area

The incomparable cellar with museum holdings at the Forge, 432 Arthur Godfrey Road, Miami Beach.

LOS RANCHOS
Nicaraguan/Miami

Once you become expert in distinguishing the difference between Cuban and Spanish dishes, it's time to tackle the Nicaraguans at Bayside, at Los Ranchos . Order churrasco beef barbecue with its trio of sauces—an onion-pepper- ketchup marinara, pickled onion cebollito and the pesto-like chimichurri made with garlic and parsley in olive oil. Alongside should be red beans and rice, gallo pinto. Put out the fire with some Nicaraguan tres leches. Try it! Believe me, you'll like it.

Bayside Marketplace, 401 Biscayne Boulevard. (305) 375-8188. Inexpensive to moderate. Lunch and dinner.

LOUISIANA RESTAURANT
American/Coral Gables

A bit of a sleeper even though the owners have been feeding Gableites since the 60s, first in the Whiffenpoof when that was practically the only hot spot in town, and since 1987 in this Victorian-accented setting where the cassoulets, the banana-braced red snapper, the duckling reposing on a bed of sliced apples and doused with fresh strawberry sauce are definitely not from the back bayous.

1630 Ponce de Leon. (305) 445-0481. Moderate. Lunch and dinner.

LULU'S ★
American/South Miami Beach

The second floor of this nostalgia-loaded bit of fun is a mini-Graceland with all kinds of Elvis memorabilia. Sit upstairs or down and feast on good burgers, spicy chicken wings, smothered pork chops, catfish and okra fritters, meat loaf and mashed potatoes, and of course fried peanut butter and banana sandwiches—Elvis' favorite.

1053 Washington Avenue. (305) 532-6147. Inexpensive. Lunch and dinner.

LYON FRERES
French/South Miami Beach

Located in the heart of historic Lincoln Road Mall, a perfect place for people-watching, this French market has wonderful salads, pre-wrapped and made-to-order sandwiches, terrific breads, cookies, brownies, and espresso bar, enjoy inside or take out to the sidewalk tables.

600 Lincoln Road. (305) 534-0600. Moderate. Breakfast, lunch and dinner.

MAIKO
Japanese/South Miami Beach

A popular place with a little sushi bar so you can start with some artfully prepared rice-wrapped rolls, little slabs of tuna, dolphin, marlin, conch or octopus. The grilled fillets of fresh fish are excellent, as are the teriyaki and sukiyaki preparations.

1255 Washington Avenue. (305) 531-6369. Moderate. Lunch and dinner.

MALAGA
Spanish/Miami

With some of the best Spanish food on Calle Ocho, Malaga is where I take the cognoscenti who want a little weekend Flamenco entertainment with their arroz con pollo and paella. The shows are professional and the ownership proud of its product.

740 South West 8th Street. (305) 858-4224. Moderate. Lunch and dinner.

MANDARIN GARDEN
Chinese/Coconut Grove

The best—and oldest—place for Hunan, Mandarin and Szechuan treats in the Grove is Mandarin Garden which is not much to look at but it is family friendly—and affordable.

3268 Grand Avenue. (305) 446-9999. Inexpensive. Lunch and dinner.

MARK'S PLACE ★★★★
New American/North Miami

Mark Militello was the first of the South Florida chefs to reach the stratosphere of national fame and only a few bites of anything from his changed-daily menu will convince you the recognition is fully justified. His new Florida cuisine hits the mark with 15 to 20 starters, a half dozen pasta and pizza choices and twice as many entrees. Our dream meal here commences with oxtail soup and marrow flan, a warm lobster salad, shrimp brulee or some "sexed-up pan seared sea scallops with wild mushroom salad and foie gras." That's followed by sesame-coated seared tuna with jasmine rice, tangerine ponzu, wakami and wasabi, or sauteed mutton snapper with a macadamia-mango-mint-ginger spiked rum brown butter, with West Indian pumpkin and coconut milk steamed rice on the side. The wine list is superb and the front room staff, starting with the marvelous hostess, is terrific.

Sans Souci Shops, 2286 Northeast 163rd Street. (305) 893-6888. Expensive. Lunch and dinner.

THE MAYFAIR GRILL
Continental/Coconut Grove

Located in the ultra-posh Mayfair House Hotel is this refuge, replete with too much glittering elegance but with a great staff and a menu that is anything but boring—lump crab fritters with spicy black beans and fried leek, polenta lasagna with salmon and scallion sauce, barley risotto with grilled sea scallops, pepper-seared tuna with Chinese vegetables and ponzu sauce, veal medallions with basil-enhanced stone crab sauce. Good wine list.

Mayfair House Hotel, 3000 Florida Avenue. (305) 441-0000. Expensive. Breakfast, lunch and dinner.

Best Nouvelle Cuban

Nobody is having more fun with the classics than the gang at YUCA, 177 Giralda Avenue, Coral Gables.

MEZZANOTTE
Italian/South Miami Beach

One night owner Piero Filpi turned up the volume of the Latin beat music and Voila! the guests started dancing on the chairs and tables. The rest is high decibel history—the only place in town where the girls dance on tables with their clothes on. The Northern Italian menu is very good and so is the wine list—start with some calamari or scampi, proceed to the pasta Dolce Vita, followed by medallions of veal and finish with one of the eye-riveting desserts.

1200 Washington Avenue. (305) 673-4343. Inexpensive. Dinner.

MONTY'S STONE CRAB
Seafood/Coconut Grove

The happy hour crowds, those who think beer when they rally for the early evening attitude readjustment confrontations, wind up here where the palm frond-covered picnic tables under the trees provide the best of casual raw bar settings for slurping freshly-shucked bivalves and cracking stone crab claws. In Florida's May 15—October 15 off season, Monty flies the claws in from South America.

2550 South Bayshore Drive. (305) 858-1431. Inexpensive to moderate. Lunch and dinner.

NEWS CAFE
American/South Miami Beach

Actually sells newsstand stuff, but this always-packed institution also sells sidewalk location and round the clock food. It's the best base camp for a marvelous melange of models and film crews, munching on the eye-popping salads—our favorite mixes calamari and spinach—bagels with Nova and cream cheese, steak tartar or meat loaf. The speakeasy style Back Room has jazz, blues, dancing and a cafe menu Wednesday through Saturday evenings.

Boulevard Hotel, 800 Ocean Drive. (305) 538-6397. Inexpensive. Breakfast, lunch and dinner.

OSTERIA DEL TEATRO ★★
Italian/South Miami Beach

The teatro is the Cameo next door but the real performances to watch take place here where chef-partner Antonion Tettamanzi executes to perfection all the nuances of the nuova Cucina school, delivered with panache by maitre d'-partner Dino Pirola. Among our favorite meals are those built around spinach noodles in a delicate ricotta-tomato sauce, asparagus with a bracing gorgonzola salute, arugula-wrapped tournedos enlivened with garlic and peppers. The wine list, with a fine inventory of the best of Gaja labels, is superb.

1443 Washington Avenue. (305) 538-7850. Expensive. Dinner.

Best Japanese Restaurant – Miami Area

Twirl your chopsticks at Toni's Sushi Bar, 1208 Washington Avenue, South Miami Beach.

RAMIRO'S
Spanish/Coral Gables

Boredom-breaking liberties are taken with the food of the mother country here where the sauces are superior and the grilling masterful—thanks to owner-chef Benito del Cueto who cooks Spanish with continental flair and finesse. He stocks a good selection of Spanish wines.

2700 Ponce de Leon, 443-7605. Moderate to expensive. Lunch and dinner.

RESTAURANT SAINT MICHEL ★★★
New American/Coral Gables

Executive chef Curtis Whitticar does not get all the fluff and puff of the over-hyped Mango Mafia chefs in South Florida but he is certainly worthy of considerable praise and serious attention. Among his many achievements, we've found good reason to applaud his herb and pepper-encrusted lamb loin with wild mushrooms and fresh thyme; braised leg and grilled duck breast in a natural berry-beautiful sauce; chicken breast rubbed with cumin and cilantro, then grilled and served with a black bean-corn-tomato salsa; roast poblano chile filled with goat cheese; and such fantastic finishers as terrine of Belgium chocolate with mango-raspberry coulis. The service is super solicitous and the setting is Art Deco inside a Mediterranean shell. There's nightly piano music and a trio playing during the superb Sunday brunches.

Hotel Place Saint Michel, 162 Alcazar Avenue. (305) 444-1666. Moderate to expensive. Breakfast, lunch, dinner and Sunday brunch.

RIVIERA KITCHEN AND BAR ★
American/South Miami Beach

This is a mission to the southern provinces by owner Tony Goldman whose SoHo kitchen and bar is the best wine bar in New York City. Here too he has wine "flights", the opportunity to taste several varieties and vintages as part of the dining experience, which is built around humungeous portions of pasta, grilled chicken and seafood, hummus and tabouleh. The sidewalk setting is super and the staff is very user-friendly.

Imperial House Hotel, 650 Ocean Drive. (305) 534-WINE. Moderate. Lunch and dinner.

RODEO GRILL
Brazilian/Coral Gables

Half fine food and half theater—and all fun as the staff moves among the tables parading skewered slabs of a dozen different cuts of meat. You do the selecting and the swordsman does the cutting and broiling. If that Tarzan act doesn't appeal, you can fall back on salmon, shrimp and snapper. Enjoy the piped-in Brazilian music. You'll want to dance a Bossa Nova.

2120 Ponce de Leon. (305) 44R-ODEO. Moderate. Lunch and dinner.

SHABEEN COOKSHACK & BAR
Jamaican/South Miami Beach

Here's a Hey Mon dive, a Shabeen, which is Jamaican for dive, a place where Jamaican chefs jerk the meats and seafood, adding with discretion their native accents— allspice, cinnamon and habanero, the hottest of peppers. We like the oxtails, the chicken, mango ice cream, the juice bar with its freshness and the fun colors of the setting in a hotel owned by Jamaican-born Island Records chief Chris Blackwell—his recording studio is upstairs from the dive.

1200 Collins Avenue. (305) 673-8373. Inexpensive to moderate. Lunch and dinner.

SHULA'S STEAK HOUSE
American/Miami Lakes

If the name sounds familiar you're a Miami Dolphins fan. Coach Don Shula has his name all over Miami Lakes. You can play a round at Shula's Golf Resort or work up a sweat at Shula's Athletic Club inside Shula's Hotel, lunch at Shu's All-Star Cafe and dine at Shula's Steak House where the football shaped menu features Shula-size steaks.

Northwest 154th Street. (305) 822-2324. Moderate to expensive. Breakfast, lunch and dinner.

SOBE BAR AND ROTISSERIE
American/Miami Beach

This latest of the Manhattan transfers to South Beach is a southern spinoff of owner Ture Tufvesson's Amsterdam restaurants in New York City. Rotisserie chicken is the specialty but they also do respectable pasta and seafood, and the indoor-outdoor setting is attractive.

560 Washington Avenue. (305) 531-7170. Moderate. Lunch and dinner.

SOREN'S FOOD AMONG THE FLOWERS
Continental/Coral Gables

For all the frustrated florists in your group, there's horticultural happiness in the garden of chef-owner Soren Bredahl. Plus great pleasure for the gastronomes as they work through Soren's specialties, nutty peach surrounded salmon, roquefort-garlic encased strip sirloin, and pepper duck Indiana Jones which translates to five kinds of pepper, corn sauce and wild rice—maybe that should be Minnesota Jones.

2728 Ponce de Leon. (305) 441-9393. Expensive. Lunch and dinner.

SOUTH POINTE SEAFOOD
Seafood/South Miami Beach

This rustic ragamuffin sits at the southern tip of South Beach with its sensational views of the Miami skyline and the ships gliding in and out of the Cruise Capital of the World. Seafood is the specialty here and management strives to find and serve the best available in markets far and near.

South Pointe Park, 1 Washington Avenue. (305) 673-1708. Moderate. Lunch and dinner.

THE STRAND ★★
American/South Miami Beach

The setting is sophisticated, the service respectful, and the kitchen quietly accommodating without a lot of hype or hoop-la. Weight watchers can concentrate on the menu that gives calorie counts for the fresh fish fillets, grilled free range chicken with vegetables and other diet food for the models. We like the steaks, the marvelous meat loaf and the perfect pecan pie.

671 Washington Avenue. (305) 523-2340. Moderate. Lunch and dinner.

THAI TONI ★
Thai/South Miami Beach

Toni is short for Hiromi Takarada who brings Bangkok to the beach with gusto, creating one of the best-dressed of the hundred or so South Florida places to Thai one on. Here's a reliable spot to order ginger-crusted whole red snapper with its peppery taste, curried shrimp or chicken in coconut milk and such palate-awakeners as satay, mee grob, and jumping squid.

890 Washington Avenue. (305) 538-8424. Moderate. Lunch and dinner.

TOBACCO ROAD
American/Miami

Despite all the present-day cosmopolitan internationalism and the mod-mod buildings, Miami was not born yesterday. This sturdy survivor opened its doors in 1912. It's a tavern where you can check out the history while trying to get your mouth around fully stacked sandwiches or forking into a fillet of fish, making plans to come back later in the evening for the blues sessions.

626 South Miami Avenue. (305) 374-1198. Inexpensive to moderate. Lunch and dinner.

TONI'S SUSHI BAR
Thai/South Miami Beach

Thai Toni-owner Hiromi Takarada is responsible for this raw bar refresher where he's devised a series of original rolls—Alaska and California Rainbow, Pink Lady and Bagel. He also serves such escapes for those who don't travel the sushi-sashimi route as sauteed duckling with a scallion-dotted shitake sauce.

1208 Washington Avenue. (305) 673-9368. Moderate. Lunch and dinner.

Best Hotel Dining – Miami Area

Nothing's grander than the Grand Cafe in the Grand Bay Hotel, 2669 South Bayshore Drive, Coconut Grove.

TUTTI'S
Italian/Coral Gables

This has all the signs of being one of the first links in a chain that's just aching to be born, but it's fun with its oversize center stage bar and open kitchen. At night there's rotisserie chicken, lasagna layered with ricotta and spinach-surrounded steak. At noon we like the large salads, seafood tangled with pasta, pizza, and at any time, the grilled fresh vegetables and the sprightly serving crew.

4612 South Le Jeune Road. (305) 663-0077. Moderate. Lunch and dinner.

THE TWO SISTERS ★★
Spanish/American/Coral Gables

An Americanized Spanish class hotel signature room with the usual handsome Hyatt accouterments, hand-painted china, gleaming silver flatware, lead crystal and an on-view kitchen. They turn out terrific tapas, along with warm and cold luncheon salads, and dinner entrees featuring fresh fish treated to light sauces of fennel, Spanish olives, basil-vermouth broth, braised cabbage. The Sunday champagne brunch is a class act all the way.

Hyatt Regency, 50 Alhambra Plaza. (305) 441-1234. Moderate to expensive. Lunch and dinner.

UNICORN VILLAGE ★
Healthfood/North Miami Beach

Dominating an important corner of the Water Place Shops of the North Miami Beach Waterways, this comfortably designed ramble is serving the best health-conscious food for miles around and is the largest natural food restaurant and marketplace in the Southeast U.S.

3565 Northeast 207th Street. (305) 933-8829. Moderate to expensive. Lunch and dinner.

VAKHO'S ★
Greek/Coral Gables

Opa! Here's an authentic Greek restaurant, one that does a marvelous moussaka, the Athenians' answer to lasagna, plus superior spanakopita, spinach wrap-around with phyllo dough crust the thickness of air, and luscious lamb laden with garlic. The Greek salad is not the real one, not with iceberg lettuce among the ingredients, but the feta is top quality and we console ourselves with some of the superior soup and a glass or two of Retsina, Rotonda or Santorini wine, the perfect complement to the flavor of the food. Their baklava and strong, strong Turkish coffee provide proper conclusions.

1915 Ponce de Leon Boulevard. (305) 444-8444. Moderate. Lunch and dinner.

VERSAILLES
Cuban/Miami

A bustling bistro on Calle Ocho that almost never closes. An oasis for the Cuban community and a Mecca for the gringos who want to experience the joys of roast pork, fried plantains, black beans, white rice, flan followed by the obligatory little cup of Cuban coffee. You can have a quick coffee fix at their take-out window while watching the world go by in Little Havana.

3555 Southwest 8th Street. (305) 445-7614. Inexpensive to moderate. Lunch and dinner.

VICTOR'S CAFE
Cuban/Miami

This enclave of tropical elegance on the south side of downtown is a spinoff from Manhattan's numero uno Cuban restaurant of the same name. They do interesting things with shrimp and filet mignon and salute snapper with Basque sauces. The service is solicitous, but some of the locals complain about the prices and remain loyal to the many Cuban cafes that were here before the carpetbaggers arrived from New York.

2340 South West 32nd Avenue. (305) 445-1313. Moderate. Lunch and dinner.

WPA RESTAURANT & BAR
American/South Miami Beach

Remember the New Deal alphabet soup agencies? This value for the money hideaway does, with kind to the wallet prices, a wall-filling mural of WPA workers, and a brownie sundae loaded with pecans and pralines called WPA. But before you order that hi-cal extravaganza, try the grilled apple-chicken sausage, a Greek salad, or an FDR burger.

685 Washington Avenue. (305) 534-1684. Inexpensive to moderate. Lunch and dinner.

YUCA ★
Cuban/Coral Gables

Here is the headquarters for Young Upward mobile Cuban Americans and anyone else who wants radical relief from the Cuban-American norm. The kitchen loves to experiment, finding all kinds of variations on the same old themes. They've come up with some real New Cuban departures— plantain-coated dolphin in a tamarind sauce, tamales peppered with conch, barbecue ribs in guava sauce served with yuca chips, and other surprises.

177 Giralda Avenue. (305) 444-4448. Expensive. Lunch and dinner.

Best French Restaurant – Miami Area

Gallic glories all the way at Le Festival, 2120 Salzedo Street, Coral Gables.

ZIO LUIGI'S
Italian/South Miami Beach

We're grateful to Uncle Luigi for having a good enough restaurant to end our Dade County selections on a happy, as well as end-of-alphabet, note. Start here with fried calamari before zeroing in on a pizza straight from the wood-burning oven. For the right kind of climax what could be better than one of Luigi's sherbets?

1137 Washington Avenue. (305) 531-8992. Inexpensive. Dinner.

Ft. Lauderdale Area Restaurants

This section lists in alphabetical order 294 restaurants in Broward County. Restaurants in the following cities are listed.

Cooper City
Coral Springs
Dania
Davie
Deerfield Beach
Fort Lauderdale
Hallandale
Hillsboro Beach
Hollywood
Lauderdale-by-the-Sea

Lauderdale Lakes
Lauderhill
Lighthouse Point
Margate
Oakland Park
Plantation
Pompano Beach
Sunrise
Tamarac
Wilton Manors

ACAPULCO LINDO
Mexican/Spanish/Fort Lauderdale

Ole! Amigos—here's a South of the Border cantina with very good beans and rice, shredded and chopped beef, the kind that goes into ropa vieja and palomilla. The tostadas and tamales are also ahead of the pack.

2361 Wilton Drive. (305) 561-5151. Inexpensive. Lunch and dinner.

ALCEO
Italian/Pompano Beach

Family-run feeder and consistent performer whether you order fried mozzarella served with a good marinara sauce, the made-out-back gnocchi, sauteed snapper or veal Alceo which means mushrooms, prosciutto and mozzarella layered on medallions.

1340 North Federal Highway. (305) 786-0004. Moderate. Dinner.

Best Oceanfront Setting

Sea Watch with its fascinating gallery of prints, paintings, portraits and nautical artifacts, 6002 North Ocean Boulevard, Fort Lauderdale.

ALIVE AND WELL
Healthfood/Davie

The best-dressed natural food feeder in the county with wonderful wood burning brick oven, multi-grain crust pizzas layered with eggplant, veggies, grilled portobellos and onions—anything but mozzarella and sausage. The grilled dolphin with soy miso and ginger is superb as are the penne tangled with broccoli and roasted garlic and served on baby wild greens, the pan-seared blackened salmon, even the To-Fu Yung cutlet made with snow peas, bamboo shoots and water chestnuts. The organic brown rice and steamed veggies are excellent, the desserts heavenly and they believe that wine is essential to good health—the list is OK.

3414 South University Drive. (305) 475-2244. Moderate. Lunch and dinner.

THE AMBRY
American/Fort Lauderdale

Gerd Mueller, German soccer star who holds the record for goals scored in World Cup competition, is immortalized here in plaques, medals and photos as well as the menu. The German chef makes sure there's always German potato salad on the salad bar, and that the menu features sauerbraten and schnitzels, a wurst or too mit kraut. But it's primarily a steak house, and a darn good one, that serves grilled chicken and seafood as well. Gott sei Dank! for Gerd.

3016 East Commercial Boulevard. (305) 771-7342. Moderate to expensive. Dinner.

AMERICO'S
Italian/Fort Lauderdale

A veteran restauranting family is in charge of this cut crystal—chandelier, red, black and gold bit of baroque and they produce reliable headliners from the American-Italian repertoire: veal marsala and Francese, chicken cacciatore, fettuccine Alfredo, cannolis and cheesecake for finishers.

2222 North Ocean Boulevard. (305) 563-4351. Moderate to expensive. Dinner.

ANDREWS DINER
American/Fort Lauderdale

If you're really worried about the amount of discretionary income available for dining, breakfasting or lunching, consider this family feeder which tries hard to live up to its boast of having "Homemade Food At Homemade Prices." You can start saving money at 6 a.m. with budget breakfasts.

2980 North Andrews Avenue. (305) 563-3555. Inexpensive. Breakfast, lunch and dinner.

ANTHONY'S RUNWAY 84
American/Fort Lauderdale

Before settling into dinner built around the kind of Americanized Italian eating New Yorkers love, check into the lounge and look out those fake airplane windows to make you think you're off on another trip to the wild blue and beyond. It all adds to the felicitous family feeling of the place.

330 State Road 84. (305) 467-8484. Moderate. Lunch and dinner.

THE ARK
American/Davie

Come by twos, threes, fours or singly to partake of the surprisingly solid offerings in this land-locked vessel which keeps the Noah nonsense to a minimum. We like the salad bar, the buffet at lunch, the prime rib, the handling of shrimp and scallops, as well as the friendliness and competence of the staff.

6255 Stirling Road. (305) 584-3075. Moderate. Lunch and dinner.

ARMADILLO CAFE ★★★★
Southwest American/Davie

The terrific twosome of Eve Montella and Kevin McCarthy are in charge of this simple little cafe with armadillos, cacti and lots of smiles for decor, and a menu featuring the finest from the Southwest. We have never been disappointed when trying any of the nightly specials, but find it hard not to order the corn-freckled, jalapeno-fired fritters, smoked duck, cedar-planked salmon, and the bourbon-spiked pecan pie peppered with chocolate chips.

4630 Southwest 64th Avenue. (305) 791-4866. Expensive. Dinner.

ARUBA BEACH CAFE
Seafood/Lauderdale-By-The-Sea

Caribbean cafe with sensational location smack on the sand overlooking fishing pier and all those body-bronzers. We start our meals here with ceviche and conch fritters, building up to pasta tangled with seafood, a freshly- assembled salad or one of their bountiful burgers. Specialty drinks and various early evening festivities add to the island spirits.

One Commercial Boulevard. (305) 776-0001. Inexpensive to moderate. Lunch and dinner.

AUGUST MOON
Chinese/Hollywood

In our favorite dim sum restaurants in New York and London we pay the bill according to the number of empty plates on the table when we finish choosing from the endless procession of delicacies—and not so delicate, such as pig skin and yellow chicken claws. Here it's not quite so dramatic, as you order from a special dim sum list, ticking off the goodies one by one, preparing for the parade of appetizers. The other food is OK but we seldom get past the starters.

1301 North Federal Highway. (305) 923-4233. Inexpensive. Lunch and dinner.

AUSTIN'S
American/Fort Lauderdale/Coral Springs

The beginnings of a chain with a clone as far afield as Orlando's International Drive. Ribs and barbecue chicken are the headliners, but they also have prime rib and hickory-grilled fillets of salmon. We like to start with the Rio Grande spinach-artichoke-cheese dip, just begging for those warm tortilla chips, and the colossal onion dubbed the Cactus Flower.

2948 Federal Highway, Fort Lauderdale, (305) 563-2556; 1203 University Drive, Coral Springs, (305) 755-0110. Moderate to expensive. Dinner.

BAHIA CABANA
American/Fort Lauderdale

Come by boat, come by land, sit under the chickee palm fronds or out on the patio picnic tables, but come casual—shorts, swimsuits, bikinis, whatever—and use the pool if you want, in between sips and snacks on conch fritters and salads, burgers and mouth-stretching sandwiches, all the while enjoying the sensational view—it's one of the best waterfront escapes in the country and it's been packing 'em in since 1972.

3001 Harbor Drive. (305) 524-1555. Inexpensive. Breakfast, lunch and dinner.

BANANA GROVE
Jamaican/Fort Lauderdale

Hey Mon! Here's the place for Jamaican jerk chicken and pork, peas and rice, fried plantains, Caribbean curries, oxtail and spicy snapper, the whole fish covered with okra, onions and tomatoes. The setting is island simple and the service is all smiles, starting with owners Shirley and Pedrol Bowen.

2941 West Sunrise Boulevard. (305) 791-6719. Inexpensive. Lunch and dinner.

BANGKOK ROOM
Thai/Pompano Beach

Thimble-size treat affably served and doing what the Thais do best, sauteeing squid with garlic and green onion bound with egg and spiked with black peppercorns; deep-frying whole red snapper enhanced mightily with chili and garlic sauce, dousing duck with curry.

900 East Atlantic Boulevard. (305) 785-5055. Moderate. Lunch and dinner.

BAVARIAN VILLAGE ★★
German/Hollywood

Owner George Zinkler knows his gemeutlichkeit, painting entry walls with Alpine scenery, outfitting his staff in Bavarian costumes, using entertainers to work the crowd and serenade the ladies, installing a menu from Munich—lots of wursts and pork, sauerbraten served with potato pancakes and launched with German beer, followed by strudel. Herr Zinkler! You are Wunderbar!

1401 North Federal Highway. (305) 922-7321. Moderate to expensive. Lunch and dinner.

BENIHANA OF TOKYO
Japanese/Lauderdale-By-The-Sea

Is there anyone out there who has not been to one of these Japanese steak houses to watch those super ambidextrous Samurai warriors wave and chop before your very eyes while seated side-by-side with strangers who insist on telling you about their Honda, Isuzu, their Sony, their trip to Tokyo?

4343 West Tradewinds Avenue. (305) 776-0111. Expensive. Dinner.

Best Pastry Cart

The stacks of sweet and creamy everything at The French Quarter, 215 southeast 8th Avenue, Fort Lauderdale.

BETTY'S
Soul Food/Fort Lauderdale

Looking for real Southern fried chicken, beef stew, smothered pork chops and sauce-slathered barbecued pork ribs, served with the right kind of fix-ins—candied yams, collard greens, corn bread, all of it made with liberal doses of TLC and lots of soul? This is the place my brothers and sisters.

601 Northwest 22nd Road. (305) 583-9121. Inexpensive. Lunch and dinner.

THE BIG APPLE
Italian/Pompano Beach

Not named for that dance craze of the 1930s, but for Fun City, depicted in a fine mural on one of the walls, across from a harbor scene of the Old Country. A model of attentive maintenance in an otherwise unkempt string of stores, this is a family-run friendly and concerned trattoria with endless varieties of pizza and pasta, plus excellent shrimp Francese and veal cacciatore.

Crystal Lake Plaza, 843 West Sample Road. (305) 941-6191. Inexpensive to moderate. Lunch and dinner.

BIMINI BOATYARD
American/Fort Lauderdale

What fun this waterfront wonder is, served by a sprightly, crew bringing such treats as grilled swordfish and Greek salads, smoked turkey, tarragon-chicken and Black Forest ham sandwiches, Jamaican jerk ribs and fried catfish. On Fridays when the singles swarm, it's the hottest action in town. We like the island feeling, the outdoor bars and the firm but friendly supervision of a vigorous staff.

1555 Southeast 17th Street. (305) 525-7400. Moderate. Lunch and dinner.

BISTRO MEZZALUNA ★★★
Italian/Fort Lauderdale

After a spell in the Dominican Republic, chef-owner Ulrich Koepf returned to the scene of his previous triumphs to open this casual comfort zone with a fine wine list, OK service and such Koepf captivators as cilantro-flavored Maryland crab cakes with ancho-grilled pepper sauce and black bean-corn-tomato salsa; swirly gemellini pasta with ground spicy sausage sprinkled with oregano; breaded chicken paillard on arugula and radicchio, a 16-ounce veal chop with roasted garlic in a red wine sauce.

741 Southeast 17th Street Causeway. (305) 522-6626. Expensive. Lunch and dinner.

BLACK BEANS BISTRO
Cuban/Davie

Another proof positive that the Cubans are moving north from Miami's Little Havana is this budget-pleasing spot which opened in mid-1993 and offers all the classics of the Cuban kitchen, starting with the Moors and Christians otherwise known as black beans and white rice. The sandwiches are superb and the arroz con pollo dinners as good as the pounded steak and roast pork.

Atrium Center, 4801 South University Drive. (305) 434-9093. Inexpensive. Breakfast, lunch and dinner.

BLUE GOOSE CAFE
Continental/Pembroke Pines

A real sleeper serving everything but blue goose: three dozen entrees including made-out-back farinaceous delights, ravioli stuffed with lobster and dressed in the three colors of the Italian flag, lamb chops, duckling, and a version of the classic carpetbagger steak using escargot instead of oysters.

Palm Plaza, 1491 North Palm Avenue (100th Avenue). (305) 436-8677. Moderate. Dinner.

BON APPETIT
Italian/Fort Lauderdale

Run by the same successful team responsible for Pompano Beach's La Veranda, this spring-bright, friendly place is a good spot for romantic rendezvousing, and for enjoying well-prepared veal Milanese, Dover sole meuniere, shrimp fra diavolo, steak given the au poivre and pizzaiola treatments.

3051 East Commercial Boulevard. (305) 776-0258. Moderate to expensive. Dinner.

BONGUSTO
Italian/Fort Lauderdale

A one-room affair large enough to give owner-chef Antonio Cerone plenty of space to present the products of his genius—mussels sauteed with garlic and scallions suspended in a heavy cream sauce, butterfly pasta tangled with primavera veggies in a pink embrace, prime veal rolled around spinach and fontina, veal shanks carved tableside, stuffed veal chop, and for grand climax, some of the best ricotta cheesecake we've ever tasted.

5640 North Federal Highway. (305) 771-9635. Moderate to expensive. Dinner.

BOODLES GRILL
Continental/Dania

An upscale operation in all aspects, from the formal, dramatically designed rooms to the professional performances by the wait staff, from the neighboring lounge with its happy hour attractions and dance club atmosphere, to the quality of food. We are particularly fond of the smashing Sunday brunch, with over half a hundred items on the groaning boards, with complimentary champagne and made before your very eyes omelets.

Sheraton Design Center Hotel, 1825 Griffin Road (at I-95). (305) 920-3500. Expensive. Dinner and Sunday brunch.

BRASSERIE MAX
American/Plantation

Paris brasserie in spirit and setting, but Cal-Italia in menu with such starters as a spinach and three-cheese melange topped with sour cream, chopped bacon and onion for dipping with blue and gold tortilla chips; and entrees like grilled salmon on spinach with warm honey-mustard dressing; hoisin barbecue pork loin with snowpeas on a hoagie roll; oak-grilled pizzas, and three standout desserts—turtle pie made with masses of nuts and chocolate bits, an almond basket filled with berries, and butterscotch pie.

Fashion Mall, 321 North University Drive. (305) 424-8000. Moderate to expensive. Lunch and dinner.

BRAVO MARIANO
Italian/Fort Lauderdale

Mariano, the maitre d'-manager-partner of this brick trattoria, used to be the front man at Il Mulino on Sunrise, which serves the same kind of Americanized Italian food—lotsa pasta, snapper Florentine, meaning with spinach, veal with a light lemon sauce, and pizzas with such names as Mona Lisa, La Deliziosa, L'Amore Mio. We like the Il Toscano Calzone and the cannolis.

1515 Southeast 17th Street Causeway. (305) 523-9441. Moderate. Lunch and dinner.

BRAZILIAN TROPICANA RESTAURANT
Brazilian/Pompano Beach

Searching for fried manioc? Bolinho de Bacalhau, Camarao Frito, Mariscada, Churrasco na Tabua, or Frango a Mineira? The dried codfish croquettes, garlic shrimp, shellfish platter, grilled meats, chicken stew are all here, prepared by a Portuguese/Brazilian kitchen watched over by owners Maria and Fernando Pestana. There's live entertainment with lots of bossa nova and girls from Impanema.

410 North Federal Highway. (305) 781-1113. Moderate. Dinner.

BREAD OF LIFE CAFE
Healthfood/Fort lauderdale

Mecca for vegetarians and other be-good-to-your-body advocates who can shop for take-out goodness and goodies after they eat, everything from vitamins and kelp to Birkenstock sandals, in the county's largest organic produce market.

Capital Bank Plaza, 2388 North Federal Highway. (305) 565-7423. Moderate. Lunch and dinner.

Best Mother-Son-Act

Hostess Pauline and chef Billy Bokis at Piccolo Cafe, 3000 Plaza, 3000 North Federal Highway, Fort Lauderdale.

BRICK OVEN PIZZERIA
Italian/Lauderhill

Is there room for one more pizzeria tucked into a simple take-out, eat-in space? Yes, if the ovens are real brick burning real wood and the pies are all individual size with thin crusts at the base and thick around the edges, topped with freshness and prepared with lots of gusto.

7100 Hollywood Boulevard, (305) 962-8822. Inexpensive. Lunch and dinner. No credit cards accepted.

BROADWAY DINER
American/Sunrise

New York deli in a diner where you can stretch the dining-out dollars along with your mouth, encircling the sandwiches, munching the salads and working through the dinners featuring the kind of fare that's now so back-to-the-basics trendy, the nouvelle grandma stuff like meatloaf and mashed potatoes.

6096 West Oakland Park Boulevard. (305) 572-3961. Inexpensive. Breakfast, lunch and dinner.

BROOKS   ★★★★
Continental/Deerfield Beach

Restauranting perfectionist Bernard Perron with wife Kathy and the second generation of Lisa Perron Howe, Jon and Marc Howe and Jean Philippe Gaudree, is a paragon in the business, always seeking to improve, to innovate. Menus shift seasonally, but we count our blessings when he has on that menu veal Normande with apples and Calvados; pan-seared shrimp spiked with Pernod; crisp duckling dressed with a sauce made from bing cherries, English mustard, port and red currant jelly. The desserts are platonic, especially the apple tart, rhubarb-strawberry crisp, pecan pie with banana ice cream—churned out back of course.

500 South Federal Highway. (305) 427-9302. Expensive. Dinner.

BURT AND JACK'S
American/Fort Lauderdale

The Burt here is none other than moneyman Burt Reynolds who would be hard put to find a more fascinating location to invest his bucks, a pseudo-Spanish mission perched on a point of land overlooking all the action at Port Everglades. Entrees are displayed in the raw during the waiter's show and tell and we can recommend the smoked salmon and lobster cocktail, lamb chops, baked chicken and New York strip sirloins.

Berth 23, Port Everglades. (305) 522-5225. Moderate to expensive. Dinner.

BUSHWHACKER'S DOWN UNDER
American/Fort Lauderdale

Opened in June, 1992, this Aussie Steak House & Pub, as they dub themselves, has a camp of Koala bears cuddling by the 100-foot Laughing Kookaburro Bar where Fosters is on tap and they pour Koala mineral water—near the dart boards and pool tables. The booth-filled dining room with a great salad bar has a stir-fry station woking up a storm of veggies and chicken. Follow that with a Bush or Boomerang burger, Joey and Boomer brewed-out-back soups, Walkabout Wings, Great Barrier Ribs, and Aussie chips on the side—they're served with a good honey-maple dip.

1620 North Federal Highway. (305) 561-4444. Inexpensive to moderate. Lunch and dinner.

BY WORD OF MOUTH
American/Fort Lauderdale

What started as a catering and take-out service has expanded into a full-scale, though still minuscule, restaurant, serving all kinds of interesting fare, from shrimp stuffed with ginger to meatloaf cordon bleu, pastry-encased salmon, and desserts that are to die for—-found in better restaurants all along the Gold Coast. You choose your food after a close-in check of the display cases and a briefing by one of the friendly and eager-to-please staff.

3200 Northeast 12th Avenue. (305) 564-3663. Moderate to expensive. Lunch and dinner.

CAFE ARUGULA ★★★
American/Lighthouse Point

Dick and Carolanne Cingolani are the dedicated duo presenting in their little domain extremely well-prepared food that is beautifully, artistically, arranged and spans several culinary traditions. The menu changes regularly but among highlights are the Cajun crawfish strudel with gumbo sauce, the cannelloni, pecan-crusted yellowtail with seafood risotto and an innovative Frangelico nut sauce with a bit of cilantro butter. Excellent service and select wines.

3150 Federal Highway. (305) 785-7732. Expensive. Dinner.

CAFE CLAUDE ★
French/Deerfield Beach

Utilizing skills honed at the Cafe Chauveron, in both Manhattan and Miami, Lauderdale's Les Trois Mousquetaires and his own La Bonne Auberge, chef-owner Claude Pottier and his wife have created the classic cafe, one with a pleasant level of fairly formal service, and a predictable menu from coquille St. Jacques to duckling in superb sauces, escargot to rack of lamb and a stunning array of desserts. For lighter fare and more casual ambiance and prices, check out his Petite Cafe next door.

Cove Shopping Center, 1544 Southeast 3rd Court. (305) 421-7337. Moderate to expensive. Lunch and dinner.

CAFE DE PARIS ★
French/Fort Lauderdale

I never tire of telling the story. Swiss-born Louis Flemati arrives in this country to work for Restaurant Associates training waiters in New York, saves his money in the best Swiss style and moves to Fort Lauderdale. He purchases a little cafe and working around the clock, pours the profits back into the place, expanding, decorating and re-decorating, establishing his own bakery and then opening another winner, the French Quarter, a few hundred feet away. What to order? Anything. I have never been disappointed and I've been eating here since 1971 B.L.—Before Louis.

715 East Las Olas Boulevard. (305) 767-2900. Moderate to expensive. Lunch and dinner.

CAFE EUROPA
Italian/Fort Lauderdale

Pizzas, subs, salads, Italian cookies and Italian gelati, capped by good espresso from the effusive Anthony Capelli, self-proclaimed "Cappuccino King of Las Olas".

726 East Las Olas Boulevard. (305) 763-6600. Inexpensive. Lunch and dinner.

CAFE GRAZIA
Italian/Lighthouse Point

Our enthusiasm has dimmed considerably since the last guide and we have received several complaints, but they still do the Mezzo and Regolare, half and full, portions for many of their dishes, a practice I wish other restaurants would emulate, and they still handle the grill with skill, preparing shrimp and calamari and our favorite dish, the combination beef tenderloin, chicken and Italian sausage, served with good oven brown potatoes.

3850 North Federal Highway. (305) 942-7206. Moderate. Lunch and dinner.

CAFE SEVILLE
Spanish/Fort Lauderdale

The finest Spanish restaurant in Broward and Palm Beach County, the happy domain of brothers Antonio and Jose Servan, who provide in their handsomely decorated little domain, exciting introductions to the culinary masterpieces of their native country. Start with Andalucian gazpacho, shrimp sauteed in olive oil splashed with sherry and sprinkled with garlic and red pepper, or the Spanish red sausage sauteed in sherry, and then concentrate on paella or the fresh salmon in pastry with mushroom puree and spinach in a white wine-basil cream sauce. Good Spanish wines.

2768 East Oakland Park Boulevard. (305) 565-1148. Moderate to expensive. Lunch and dinner.

CAFE ST. TROPEZ   ★
Middle Eastern/Fort Lauderdale

The Armenian Alboyabgian family put their ten years' experience running a Pompano Beach grocery to good use when they opened this headquarters for falafel and hummus, tahini, gyros and tabouleh, familiar names to anyone who enjoys the cuisine of the Middle East. But they also assemble Cuban sandwiches in their storefront Mecca, along with burgers, Philly cheese-steaks and gyros made from chicken, an Alboyabgian original. My favorite food here? The lentil pilaf with chopped white onions, the Greek feta salad and the lamb shank, sliced from the bone and stacked on a plate, loaded with garlic of course.

Sunrise Square, 1201 North Federal Highway.(305) 566-6426. Inexpensive to moderate. Lunch and dinner.

CAFE 66
American/Fort Lauderdale

Great waterfront location overlooking Pier 66's marina and the Waterway, and one of our favorite lunching spots, working through a Caesar salad enhanced with pecans and smoked shrimp, fish and chips, or the day's pasta. We come back at night for early dinners structured around gravlaks, snapper consomme, spit-roasted duckling in a blackberry-orange glaze, or the sauteed swordfish with papaya fig compote and nut-flavored butter.

Pier 66 Resort, 2301 Southeast 17th Street Causeway.(305) 728-3500. Moderate to expensive. Lunch and dinner.

CAMI'S SEAFOOD PLACE
Seafood/Sunrise/Pembroke Pines/Fort Lauderdale

Rock-bottom prices for freshly-shucked oysters, freshly baked shrimp and freshly made pasta in stark surroundings served by a young, fast-moving staff. We like most the garlic shrimp cooked to order.

3549 North University Drive, Sunrise, (305) 748-8404;7996 Pines Boulevard, Pembroke Pines, (305) 987-FISH;1001 North Federal Highway, Fort Lauderdale, (305) 463-3003. Inexpensive. Lunch and dinner.

CAP'S PLACE
Seafood/Lighthouse Point

Unique in every way, starting with a boat ride from the mainland and arrival at a shack-bar where you expect to find a belching Charles Laughton or unshaven Bogie hunkered down. Spend some time reading the many articles about the history and the career of Cap Knight, then settle into hearts of palm salad, excellent fillets of broiled fish, stone crab, accompanied by some of the best French fries you'll ever put in your mouth.

Cap's Dock, 2765 Northeast 28th Court. (305) 941-0418. Expensive. Dinner.

CAPRICCIO
Italian/Pembroke Pines

Live out the name here and have a flirtation with one of the most refreshing and lovingly cared for ristorantes in South Florida, ably operated by Maitre d'-Captain-owner Gianpiero Cangelosi, who is also the guitarist-singer. Start with the antipasto array, moving into some angel hair with the heart of garlic-zapped tomato, and then order veal parmesan or zingara, meaning onions, mushrooms and peppers. All the veal entrees are noteworthy and when Florida lobster is in season, the kitchen knows exactly how to handle it.

2424 North University Drive. (305) 432-7001. Moderate to expensive. Dinner.

Best Desserts – Broward

By Word of Mouth's sinfully seductive sweets, 3200 Northeast 12th Avenue, Fort Lauderdale.

CARLOS & PEPE'S 17TH STREET CANTINA
Mexican/Fort Lauderdale

When this cantina opened in the 1970's, it was the taco talk of the town, the hot tamale, the whole enchilada. Then came a roller coaster period of problems, but now the cantina is back on track, the margaritas are OK, the cobb salad and combo plates something to consider seriously.

1302 Southeast 17th Street. (305) 467-7192. Inexpensive to moderate. Lunch and dinner.

CASA DE LUCA
Italian/Pompano Beach

Sal de Luca moved his simple little casa over from the ocean to this elaborately elegant free-standing mansion, replete with twinkling little lights everywhere, lots of black and gold and a staff that sparkles. Although Sal is from Palermo, his menu is basically Northern Italian and that means artichoke hearts in the Roman manner, veal breaded Milanese style, the lightest of sauces, good selection of Italian wines.

1184 South Federal Highway. (305) 942-1011. Expensive. Dinner.

CASANOVA ITALIAN RESTAURANT
Italian/Coral Springs

The setting of this surprise storefront is conducive to romantic trysts and the kitchen does its part with an excellent array of pasta tangled with seafood and vegetables, flattered with far better than average sauces—our favorite is anything with sun-dried tomatoes. The veal is handled with care but in season with the crowds, service can be a bit spotty.

1853 University Drive. (305) 344-1353. Moderate. Lunch (in season only) and dinner.

CASARELLA
Italian/Coral Springs

Although open since 1982 this neat little storefront is the very definition of immaculate—it looks like it opened yesterday. Pizza is the big seller, but I come here for the "Shrimp Outrageous," five luscious crescents wrapped in prosciutto and a modest amount of mozzarella sprinkled with bread crumbs crispified under the grill.

10288 West Sample Road, (305) 346-0304. Inexpensive to moderate. Lunch and dinner.

CATFISH DEWEYS
Seafood/Oakland Park

The current base camp for those who just can't say no to the schools of yaller cats that come swimming to the table, those small and medium size farm-raised fingerlings eaten like corn on the cob and accompanied by slaw, hush puppies, french fries and grits. Early in the week, there are also all-you-eat-steamed shrimp pigouts. Ultra casual and fun.

4003 North Andrews Avenue. (305) 566-5333. Inexpensive. Lunch and dinner.

Best Sushi – Broward

If you knew Sushi like I know sushi you'd run to the Japanese Village, 716 East Las Olas Boulevard, Fort Lauderdale.

THE CAVES
American/Fort Lauderdale

What else would you call a place where you actually sit in your own cave, simulated of course—what else in pool table flat South Florida? No, you're not going to be greeted by Fred Flintstone or served by Wilma and you won't have to dine on dinosaur. Fillets of broiled fish and beef are the order of the night.

2205 North Federal Highway. (305) 561-4608. Moderate. Dinner.

CHAMELEON
American/Fort Lauderdale

The menu at this four-star stunner changes like the colors of Florida's favorite lizard, and they're executed with precision and passion by chef-partners Thomas and Cynthia Fyfe, and delivered with great finesse and pride by a fine staff under the knowledgeable direction of masterful maitre d'-manager-sommelier-partner James Deering. What a team they make and what a sophisticated setting. Sensational wine list, superior cheffing with magnificient crab cakes remoulade, potted vegetable terrines, sauteed sea scallops crowned with foie gras, goat cheese-mesclun salads, veal chops with wild mushroom sauce, red snapper flattered with spinach, shitakis and Reggiano, and much, much more.

1095 Southeast 17th Street, (305) 522-6795. Expensive. Dinner.

CHARCOAL CHARLIE'S STEAK HOUSE
American/Fort Lauderdale

This landmark smoker celebrated its 42nd anniversary in 1993 by changing its name from Smoke House to Steak House. That's the trend but they're still serving barbecue, beef on a stick and all the usual fixins'— beans, fries, slaw, in a postage stamp place that has fed thousands.

1445 Northeast Fourth Avenue. (305) 462-7427. Moderate. Lunch and dinner.

CHARCUTERIE TOO
American/Fort Lauderdale

Here's a real surprise! A first class restaurant in a library, which itself is a stunner, easily one of the sights of the town, along with the Art Museum next door. The array of salads is sensational, as much a joy to look at when passing through the buffet line, as to eat. Freshly brewed soups and freshly made sandwiches are in the same winning big leagues and the muffins and desserts are to die for.

Broward County Main Library, 100 South Andrews Avenue. (305) 463-9578. Moderate. Lunch and dinner.

CHARLEY'S CRAB   ★
Seafood/Deerfield Beach/Fort Lauderdale

Here are two links of a nation-wide chain, one in the location that was forever Pal's Captains Table and the other formerly Harrison's on the Water. The menus are the same, which means excellent appetizers of black bean soup, eggplant crepe with three cheeses, seared tuna sashimi, beef carpaccio and oysters Florentine. Follow those with one of the several selections of fresh fish prepared a variety of ways, the Nantucket scallops, salmon papillote, roast pork or prime rib. Good wine selection by the glass.

1755 Southeast Third Court, Deerfield Beach, (305) 427-4000; 3000 Northeast 32nd Avenue, Fort Lauderdale, (305) 561-4800. Expensive. Lunch and dinner.

THE CHART HOUSE
American/Fort Lauderdale

Occupying two historic turn-of-the-century homes, this local outpost of the national chain that specializes in such adaptive restoration is the best-dressed restaurant for close-in pre-theater dining—the Broward Center for Performing Arts is only a few hundred yards away. Start with oysters casino or Rockefeller, New England clam chowder or lobster bisque before settling down with the teriyaki chicken, shrimp or steak, the baked scallops, Australian lobster tails or prime rib.

301 Southwest 3rd Avenue. (305) 523-0177. Expensive. Dinner.

CHECKER'S OLD MUNCHEN
German/Pompano Beach

Here's a real money saver but you have to like the wurst—the best of the wurst not the wurst of the best, and you have to hanker for schnitzels, sauerbraten, kraut and red cabbage, launched with good German beer and wine.

2209 East Atlantic Boulevard. (305) 785-7565. Inexpensive. Lunch and dinner.

CHEF LIEN'S
Chinese/Lighthouse Point

Chef Lien Lehr, a Vietnamese-born enthusiast, is the big news here, along with ever-smiling, cheerful husband Bob, who runs the front room while Lien is loading up the spring rolls, the pork and shrimp crepes, mixing the several salads, best dressed with Lien's fusion of roquefort and ranch house. Her soups are a highlight and the ginger chicken is especially noteworthy, but don't sell the duck short or the crispy whole red snapper.

Georgetown Plaza, 5020 North Federal Highway. (305) 427-5959. Inexpensive to moderate. Lunch and dinner.

CHEZ PORKY'S ★
American/Pompano Beach/Coral Springs

No one in Buffalo ever dreamed of treating chicken wings to raspberry vinaigrette, curry, lemon-garlic, barbecue and spicy Oriental sauces. Take your pick and move on to something wonderful called Caribbean coconut chicken, blackened dolphin, barbecue chicken and ribs. The first storefront in Pompano was so successful they opened a second in Coral Springs.

105 Southwest Sixth Street, Pompano Beach, (305) 946-5590; 2246 North University Drive, Coral Springs, (305) 752-7675. Inexpensive. Lunch and dinner.

CHIANG MAI OF SIAM
Thai/Fort Lauderdale

Anyone out there remember the Lum's links all over the state? They're long gone but their buildings have served as all kinds of feederies including this one which manages to keep a few feet ahead of the competition with their sizzling and spicy whole fish, curried chicken, sweet and sour shrimp, and noontime buffets.

3341 North Federal Highway. (305) 565-0855. Inexpensive to moderate. Lunch and dinner.

CHIANTI
Italian/Fort Lauderdale

Romantic escape with accommodating service, and the same kind of Italian fare found elsewhere, but within classier walls. Our favorites here are the shrimp fra diavolo, the pasta given a jolt of vodka and the veal grilled over oak, and of course, the chianti.

2831 East Oakland Park Boulevard. (305) 561-4011. Moderate to expensive. Dinner.

CHINA YUNG
Chinese/Fort Lauderdale

With all the restaurants blessing both sides of Lauderdale's Street of Good Eats, it's inevitable that the purveyors of sweet and sour pork, Lo Mein and Moo Goo Gai Pan would be represented. We come here for the dim sum, the fried dumplings filled with minced pork, the sizzled-at-the-table Seafood Wor Bar—lobster, scallops and shrimp in an egg white light creamy sauce—and the garlic beef with broccoli and snow peas. Garlic is the oldest herb recorded in history—in China thousands of years ago.

720 East Las Olas Boulevard. (305) 761-3388. Moderate. Lunch and dinner.

CHINESE FISHING VILLAGE
Chinese/Fort Lauderdale

Simple setting and no-nonsense service but with a good buffet featuring the usual—wings and ribs, egg rolls and fantail shrimp—but also shrimp in lobster sauce, honey-glazed chicken and fresh crabs stir-fried with ginger and scallion-freckled sauce. We also like the seafood harvest delivered in a steaming clay pot.

2832 Stirling Road. (305) 920-9995. Inexpensive. Lunch and dinner.

Best Thai Restaurant – Broward

Thai-one-on at Thai Spice, 1514 East Commecial Boulevard, Fort Lauderdale.

CHRISTOPHER'S
Continental/Fort Lauderdale

Cross-cultural, mixed crowd mingling of regular yuppies with the uppity yuppies plus graduate yuppies and beyond—they gather at the handsomely-appointed tables in the middle of the day for lunch and later for dinners built around steaks, grilled chicken, seafood and pastabilities, including our favorite, the tortelline Christopher with broccoli, mushrooms and shrimp in pesto sauce. Live entertainment and packed dance floor.

2857 East Oakland Park Boulevard. (305) 561-2136. Moderate. Lunch and dinner.

CHUCK'S STEAK HOUSE
American/Fort Lauderdale

Popular gathering place for beef lovers, especially those who want a steady diet of prime rib, but there's also plenty of room here for the seafood set—the grilled fillets of fish are very good, as is the salad bar—the Chuck chain invented the concept.

1207 Southeast 17th Street. (305) 764-3333. Moderate. Lunch and dinner.

CIELITO LINDO UNO, DOS, TRES ★
Mexican/Pompano Beach/Lighthouse Point/Oakland Park

What started in Pompano Beach in 1985 as the first Cielito Lindo was cloned into a trio, each serving marvelous Margaritas, superior chicken soup and stir-fry veggies with beef or chicken and a ginger sauce, crab enchiladas, shrimp creole and such Spanish favorites as arroz con pollo, the best-ever palomilla, charbroiled thin sirloin showered with chopped sweet onion and parsley and served with a crescent of lime. For Spanish tapas treats, check into the Cielito Lindo Cantina next door to Numero Dos in Lighthouse Point.

600 South Dixie Highway, Pompano Beach, (305) 782-1600;4480 North Federal Highway, Lighthouse Point, (305) 941-8226; 91 East Prospect Road, Oakland Park, (305) 776-1581. Inexpensive. Lunch and dinner.

COCONUTS
American/Fort Lauderdale

Singer John Day is responsible for this wonderful waterfront winner with indoor-outdoor decks for casual consumption of good sandwiches, chicken and tuna salads and coconut-coated shrimp. The dining room has a more ambitious menu of fresh fish and meats in some of the most generous portions to be found in Florida, climaxed by some of the most humungous desserts we've ever been privileged to encounter. Lively nightly entertainment.

429 Seabreeze Boulevard. (305) 467-6788. Moderate to expensive. Lunch and dinner.

CORAL ROSE CAFE
American/Hollywood

Straightforward, honest coffee shop in the classic American tradition, serving breakfast from 7 a.m. Wednesday through Saturday and 8 a.m. on Sunday—gathering place for local power brokers—and lunches the same days featuring heart-happy, low calorie, low fat, low sodium stuff that really has flavor—beanless turkey chili, charbroiled salmon-topped pizza, seafood quesadillas with a fine salsa and a side dish of jalapenos.

1840 Harrison Street. (305) 925-4414. Inexpensive. Breakfast and lunch.

THE COVE
American/Deerfield Beach

Overlooking the Intracoastal and a marina, with broad outside decks and bar, live entertainment and won't-quit menus offering shrimp scampi, steamed Dungeness crab, scallops Nantucket and Canadian, pasta primavera, chicken parmesan, quiche of the day, steaks, burgers and sandwiches. Their happy hour is the best for miles around and really packs in the yuppies, past, present and future.

1755 Southeast 3rd Court. (305) 421-9272. Moderate to expensive. Breakfast, lunch and dinner.

CRAB POT ★
Seafood/Pompano Beach

Who says you can't go home again? Restauranting entrepreneur Wayne Cordero did it, taking back this property and transforming it into a Chesapeake Crab House—with class. Concentrating on what he did when he started in the business in 1972—sell crabs. Hand-picked blues, steamed in beer and Old Bay seasoning, or given the garlic treatment, brought to the newspaper-covered tables for the crabophiles to pound and pick. You like the big ones, the Jimmys as they're known (there are never any Janes because the females do not grow as large)? Put your name on the Jimmy list and you'll be contacted when they come in. There's other seafood on the menu, plus all-you-can-eat specials and early bird offerings, but it's the crabs that count.

200 East McNab Road. (305) 783-5200. Moderate. Lunch and dinner.

CRAB SHANTY
Seafood/Fort Lauderadale

A new owner took over this two-story super size shanty in 1992, cleaning up the nooks and crannies, and staging all kinds of celebrations featuring Maine lobsters, Florida shrimp, Danish lobster tails and Maryland blue crabs prepared Baltimore style in Old Bay seasoning or with garlic. Land-locked appetites can console themselves with chicken and beef alternatives.

2960 North Federal Highway. (305) 564-4522. Moderate. Dinner.

CRYSTAL PALACE
Chinese/Coral Springs

Chicagoan Simon Lin, whose Szechuan House at this site was a real winner, moved back to the Windy City but retained an interest, advising from afar about their preparation of garlic shrimp, Hunan-spiced beef and chicken, sweet and sour crispy shrimp and orange beef.

Black Crystal Building, 3111 University Drive. (305) 344-8990. Moderate. Lunch and dinner.

CYPRESS NOOK
German/Pompano Beach

Unique in these parts is the split personality of this nook. Two couples run it, one pair for breakfast and lunch, the other in the evening, when we like to check in for some honest Old Country cooking, refreshed by one of the several excellent German beers available and making sure to get all the side dishes—sauerkraut, red cabbage, spaetzle, noodles, boiled or mashed potatoes. The fried cauliflower and mushrooms are a good start—crisp and greaseless—to the feasts built around pork, lamb and veal shanks, jaeger and wiener schnitzels, roast goose, vegetable plates. But remember to save room for the strudel.

201 East McNab Road. (305) 781-3464. Inexpensive to moderate. Breakfast, lunch and dinner.

THE CYPRESS ROOM
Continental/Fort Lauderdale

The smallest link in the Westin chain, but one with active, imaginative food and beverage leadership, organizing special ethnic culinary promotions in a better than average ground floor coffee shop and this far-better-than-average second floor formal dining room, one specializing in nouvelle American fare.

The Westin Cypress Creek, Interstate 95 and Cypress Creek Road East. (305) 772-1331. Expensive. Dinner.

DAKOTA'S ★
American/Margate

Down home eating, partner—country cookin' with chicken fried steak, barbecue sandwiches and ribs, catfish and southern fried chicken otherwise known as Hog Heaven, Fargo Fry, Bronc Buster, Chicken Coop, Mother Lode, Happy Hatfield and Custer's Last Clam. All dinners come with a choice of two of the 11 fixin's—including corn on the cob, mashed potatoes and gravy, baked beans and green beans, slaw, fried okra and hush puppies. In the off-season there are cowboy belt busting all-you-can-eat specials. Cookin' Country band Wednesday—Saturday. Y'all come, hear?

850 South State Road 7. (305) 968-6916. Inexpensive. Lunch (in season only) and dinner.

DANTE'S
American/Fort Lauderdale

I can't remember the time when this upscale steak house with its inviting upfront bar wasn't in business. Some of the veteran waiters might have come in with Major Lauderdale to fight the Indians. He might have been the first to pass the prime rib over the coals before serving.

2871 North Federal Highway. (305) 564-6666. Expensive. Dinner.

DARREL AND OLIVER'S CAFE MAXX ★★★★
American/Pompano Beach

The best-of-all partnerships in South Florida, super-chef Oliver Saucy and masterful manager Darrel Broek, changed their name in 1993 from Cafe Max; but they could just as well have made that Cafe Marvelous or Magnificent, so sensational is the product whisking and whirling out of Saucy's insatiable desire to innovate without falling off the culinary edge. His cross-cultural fusion fare, combining the best of all possible worlds, from the Caribbean, the Southwest, the far reaches of the Pacific, is a never-ending joy to experience. He and Darrel delight in putting together a wealth of winemaker and special celebratory dinners. The wine list and the serving staff keep pace to make this the Maxximum!

2601 East Atlantic Boulevard. (305) 782-0606. Expensive. Dinner.

DEER CREEK
American/Deerfield Beach

A public country club that looks good enough to be private, with handsomely landscaped grounds on view through dining room windows, a 19th hole bar, and the same management that makes McDivot's in Margate at the Carolina Club worth a trip. We start here with the rock shrimp blessed by an incredibly good remoulade, the Creek Blossom battered and deep-fried whole Vidalia onion or the much-better-than-average smoked fish dip. For the mains we like the poached Atlantic salmon, the scallops sauteed with broccoli and roast peppers with fresh dill on a bed of linguine or the chargrilled lamb chops marinated in rosemary.

2801 Country Club Boulevard. (305) 421-5553. Moderate. Lunch and dinner.

DOCKERS
American/Dania

This nautical-theme highway-hugger specializes in blackened dolphin, barbecue ribs, and variations on the Caesar salad theme adding seafood and chicken. Fresh catch-of-the-day is prepared any which way but frozen. In addition to the dining space there's a game room. The bar with its happy-hour buffet is a real magnet for the locals.

318 North Federal Highway. (305) 920-7072. Inexpensive to moderate. Lunch and dinner.

DOCKSIDE
American/Hollywood

Let the kids feed the amberjack and catfish while you feed your face at this accurately named bit of happily-served informality, spooning into the brewed-out-back chowders before you head into the gorgonzola cheese salad with garlic bread, burgers, steaks and great sandwiches—our favorite is built around blackened fish.

908 North Ocean Drive. (305) 922-2265. Inexpensive to moderate. Lunch and dinner.

DON ARTURO'S
Spanish-Cuban/Fort Lauderdale

What started as a simple little counter with a few tables is now a full-blown restaurant, complete with black-suited waiters, live entertainment, wine list and a kitchen turning out all the classics of Spanish cuisine as interpreted by South Florida Cuban chefs. Pork tenderloin, sherry-splashed caper-covered swordfish and garlic shrimp are my favorites.

1198 Southwest 27th Avenue. (305) 584-7966. Inexpensive. Lunch and dinner.

Best Bread – American

Check Little Red Riding Hood's basket at the 15th Street Fisheries, 1900 Southeast 15th Street, Fort Lauderdale.

DORIA'S PIER 5
Italian/Seafood/Hallandale

Convenient for racing fans who want to wind up a day of watching the ponies pound the turf at Gulfstream across the street, this is a time-honored family operation, by the Perrones, who serve pasta, consistently good seafood but also chicken and veal parmesan, steaks and lamb chops. The service is super solicitous.

126 South Federal Highway. (305) 454-2410. Moderate. Dinner.

DOWN UNDER
Continental/Fort Lauderdale

Down Under the bridge, not something Crocodile Dundee devised, and taking advantage of that location with outside waterfront patio tables, a better bet than some of the interior rooms which do get a bit loud. The menu is an eclectic one, perfected over the two decades they've been a leader on the local restaurant scene. Superb wine list and a good lunch list—in 1993 the menu was lightened, in both cost and variety; they're even serving burgers at competitive prices.

3000 East Oakland Park Boulevard. (305) 563-4123. Expensive. Lunch and dinner.

EDUARDO'S
Italian/Fort Lauderdale

Jimmy Colosimo has owned this landmark with its giant banyans shading one of our favorite courtyards since the early 1970's, but after leasing it to a string of failures, took it back in 1990, installing an Italian menu, finding a friendly crew and cleaning up the corners. Our meals are built around shrimp and scallops mingled with linguine, chicken cacciatore or veal piccata.

2400 East Las Olas Boulevard. (305) 767-0603. Moderate to expensive. Lunch, dinner and Sunday brunch.

EMILIO'S
Italian/Davie

Lively lounge with non-stop entertainment and a 30s—60s dance crowd shared the space of this massive roadhouse. The dining room is off to the left and features a solid selection of steaks and chops, prime rib, plus a parade of pasta. Order the caveman prime sirloin—it's cut at the table and charged by the ounce.

2101 South University Drive. (305) 475-2006. Dinner. Moderate.

ERNIE'S BAR-B-Q & LOUNGE
Barbecue/Fort Lauderdale

Go up to the second deck and sit under the awning to watch beautiful Federal Highway go by while you pour a little more sherry in your conch chowder, play typewriter with your corn on the cob, bite into a barbecue beef or pork sandwich on Bimini bread. Man! That's livin'.

1843 South Federal Highway. (305) 523-8636. Inexpensive. Lunch and dinner.

ERNIE'S CRAB HOUSE
Seafood/Wilton Manors

Here's the kind of combo not often found so far inland—a fish market and a fish restaurant side by side. What you see should be what you get. And you'll do the getting at great kind-to-the-wallet prices, whether you spoon conch chowder or lobster bisque, harpoon raw clams and oysters, chomp your way through the catfish or play the anvil chorus hammering the blue crabs.

2724 North Andrews Avenue. (305) 566-CRAB. Inexpensive. Lunch and dinner.

FAMOUS LEVY'S
Kosher/Sunrise

Rather immodestly or maybe that's hopefully, named, but a reliable place for kosher meals thoughtfully prepared and efficiently served at prices that do little damage to the pocketbook.

8267 Sunset Strip. (305) 742-8384. Inexpensive to moderate. Lunch and dinner.

FANTASTIC
Cuban/Hallandale

The name does not apply to the setting but to the bilingual, budget-minded everything from the Cuban kitchen—roast chicken and pork, palomilla steak, shredded beef, shrimp creole, the famous Cuban and medio noche (midnight) sandwiches and desserts of flan, guava and papaya with cream cheese.

701 West Hallandale Beach Boulevard. (305) 454-7111. Inexpensive. Lunch and dinner.

FELIX LO'S
Chinese/Hollywood

Felix moved his act from Miami to this mega-shopping strip, importing a Hong Kong dim sum chef who fills the carts on Sundays and offers check-off menu selections during the week. Among the dozen little delights we like most are the crab-filled eggplant, steamed chicken bun, shrimp dumplings in transparent skin revealing flecks of parsley, and Malaysian curry chicken with Szechuan-ginger sauce.

5301 Sheridan Street. (305) 989-7600. Inexpensive to moderate. Lunch and dinner.

Best Bouillabaisse

It's not Marseilles and there's no chapon or gurnet but it's marvelous at Froggie's, 900 East Atlantic Boulevard Pompano Beach.

15TH STREET FISHERIES ★★★
Seafood/Fort Lauderdale

Owner Mike Hurst is a seminal force in the restaurant industry, a professor in the Hotel and Restaurant School of Florida International University, noted lecturer all over the world, and activist in the National Restaurant Association which he served as president 1990-1991. How is he as a restaurateur? In a word, terrific. As a recruiter, promoter, manager and motivator, as quality controller and fresh fish purchaser, and in finding Mike Pinion to serve as clone in his absence. The setting is instant-old nautical packing house, the staff is all smiles, from barkeep to bread girl, the selection of seafood extensive and exciting and the wine choice excellent.

1900 Southeast 15th Street. (305) 763-2777. Moderate to expensive. Lunch and dinner.

FIN N' CLAW ★
Seafood/Lighthouse Point

Originally a New Jersey seafood server but in this blockhouse long enough to have built a solid reputation for seafood that is reliably fresh and respectfully handled by a very competent kitchen, which can also do Austrian and German specialties. Early bird dinners please the budgeteers and if you want to know the fresh fish of the night, the features of the week, call in advance and listen to the recorded message—"Tonight we have fresh Norwegian salmon and you can have it poached, broiled or blackened and all week there are Maine lobster dinners..."

2502 North Federal Highway. (305) 782-1060. Moderate. Dinner.

THE FISH GRILL
Seafood/Dania

The name has to be taken seriously. This is the place to find good charcoal grilled fish, snapper, salmon, dolphin,whatever the markets can supply. The grill chefs handle it with respect and it's served without complications. There are money-saving early dinners with a choice of 17 entrees and the homemade desserts are A-OK.

103 East Dania Beach Boulevard. (305) 923-1001. Inexpensive to moderate. Dinner.

FISHERMAN'S WHARF
Seafood/Pompano Beach

This ocean-hugging fishing pier shack serves reliably fresh catch of the day, good shrimp scampi and fish chowders as well as steaks, barbecued and parmesan-coated chicken. For the lunch bunch, burgers and sandwiches. Live entertainment nightly packs the adjacent lounge.

222 Pompano Beach Boulevard. (305) 941-5522. Moderate. Lunch and dinner.

FLAMING PIT
American/Pompano Beach

An uncomplicated, unpretentious solid feeder for a large legion of repeat customers who keep coming back for the friendly waitresses, the salad bar, the neatly maintained setting and the reasonably priced food.

1150 North Federal Highway. (305) 943-3484. Inexpensive. Lunch and dinner.

THE FLORIDIAN
American/Fort Lauderdale

College coffee shop setting with blackboard menu, bustling staff and carry-out cuisine headlined by the hottest conch chowder in Christendom, great chili dogs and burgers, fabulous skins-on French fries. Open at 7 a.m. for breakfasts and serving snack stuff all day long.

1410 East Las Olas Boulevard. (305) 463-4041. Inexpensive. Breakfast, lunch and dinner.

FRANK'S RISTORANTE
Italian/Pompano Beach

A classic Italian/American ristorante run by a professional crew and named for the soft-spoken, cool and collected Frank Di Maria, who started with a simple little pizzeria which is still alongside this nicely appointed ristorante, a reliable provider of pasta in most of its forms, excellent shrimp dishes, good veal with OK wines.

3428 East Atlantic Boulevard. (305) 785-4140.   Moderate. Lunch and dinner.

THE FRENCH PLACE
French/Pompano Beach

A magical recreation in setting, service and spirit of a favorite hideaway in the French-speaking provinces. Chef-owner Jean-Pierre, who bakes some of the best bread to be found in Florida, also brews very good French onion and fish soups. For starters we like the cognac-spiked terrine made from properly spiced liver or pork and the vegetable pate, and for the main action, sole meuniere, poached salmon, sweetbreads in a rich cream sauce, and the grouper Grenobloise. But most of all, we like the feeling of being back in the old country, and the wonderful staff.

360 East McNab Road. (305) 785-1920. Moderate. Lunch and dinner.

FRENCH QUARTER
French/Fort Lauderdale

Among the many reasons we keep coming back to this upscale spinoff from the nearby Cafe de Paris is the history of the home, built by the town's mayor in the 1920s, transformed to Red-Cross headquarters and utilized as refuge from hurricanes. It is a model of adaptive restoration, an interior landscaper's dream of lush greenery, with many tucked-away tables for two and an overall feeling of springtime romance. The wine room is great for private parties. There are a few New Orleans style offerings but the main thrust is French. Remember to save space for something sinfully delicious off the dessert cart.

215 Southeast 8th Avenue. (305) 463-8000. Expensive. Lunch and dinner.

FROGGIES
French/Pompano Beach

Kitchen elf Agnes and husband Rene out front make a *trés, trés magnifique* couple, providing baked daily French bread, family-size salad bowls, *tarte aux champignon* mushroom pies and trout *en papillote* that are fantastic. Tuesday means bouillabaisse and it's beautiful, but then so is everything else and so are they with all their eagerness and enthusiasm.

900 East Atlantic Boulevard. (305) 941-0906 . Moderate to expensive. Dinner.

FULVIO'S ★★★
Italian/Davie

This consistent performer started as a simple pizzeria but Fulvio was doing so many things right he expanded into a trattoria, remodeling again in the summer of '91, and now is definitely in the ristorante class, serving meals that start with prosciutto and melon or fried calamari and continue through eggplant parmesan, baked ziti, lasagna or steak pizzaiola, to finish with tartufo and tiramisu. But there are always specials of the night, predicated on his success in the market that day—luscious lamb chops, awesome osso buco, fine fillets of fresh fish. And you can special order anything. Fulvio is a chef with many talents.

4188 Southwest 64th Avenue. (305) 583-3666. Inexpensive to moderate. Dinner.

GEORGE WALES GENEVE CAFE ★
Swiss/Fort Lauderdale

In 1992 Swiss-born founder-owner Wales returned to the scene of his earlier success, where for 15 years he had carefully constructed memories of the Old Country, complete with Zermatt Bar, Swiss cow bells, posters and photographs, and a menu that yodels its way through all kinds of fondue, starters of paper-thin, air-dried bundnerfleisch and rich cream soups, to entrees of fresh trout and geschnetzeltes, or emince de veau as they say in Wales' French-speaking canton, strips of veal surrounded with cognac-spiked cream sauce. Accompanied by roesti, the special Swiss fried potatoes, of course. A great place to re-live your holidays in the Oberland or plan the next trip to the Confederation.

1519 South Andrews Avenue. (305) 522-8928. Moderate. Lunch and dinner.

Best Raw Bar

The Southport where the unwashed mingle with the mighty, 1536 Cordova Road, Fort Lauderdale.

GEORGIA PIG BAR-B-Q
Barbecue/Fort Lauderdale

Frances and Wayne, mother and son, are the Georgians—from Jesup across the border, not Tbilisi across the sea—responsible for the Brunswick stew, macaroni and potato salads, barbecue ribs, beef, chicken and pork smoked over oak in an open pit that's a highlight of the decor. If you think the sauce needs a little oomph, there's plenty of bottled fire on the tables, and I suppose those guys in the wide-brim hats bring their own datil peppers.

1285 South State Road 7, (40th Avenue). (305) 587-4420. Inexpensive. Lunch and dinner.

GIBBY'S
American/Oakland Park

Go past the warehouses until you see the country club estate mansion, an offshoot from a time-honored restaurant in Montreal. But don't expect something French, or even Canadian. This is strictly a prime rib—veal chop—steak—broiled fish—lobster tail—German chocolate cake kind of place. A high volume feeder that manages to out-point the competition, feeding guests in a series of rooms that deaden noise and provide a sense of privacy. Good wine selection.

2900 Northeast 12th Terrace. (305) 565-2929. Moderate to expensive. Lunch and dinner.

GIORGIO
Italian/Davie

When this storefront winner opened in mid-1992, it brought years of experience at GiGi's in North Miami with it. Some of the hand-crafted ceramics still carry the name and in her every action as hostess-manager, mama Maria reflects the memories and the lessons. Chicago-born husband John also helps out front along with daughter-waitress Rita, while son Mario is in charge of the kitchen and an endless menu, everything from 11 different fettuccine features to tripe sauteed in an onion-tomato sauce. Our favorite feast here, after the soup and salad served family style, is the Zuppa di Pesce—carefully selected and carefully cooked clams, mussels, scallops, grouper or snapper and superb sliced conch that's the best in the west—and east, north, south.

Carriage Hills, 6920 Stirling Road. (305) 962-0414. Moderate. Dinner.

GOLD COAST
American/Hollywood

Founder and long time operator Joe Sonken is no longer at the tiller, but he left the Chicago memories behind along with a veteran maitre d' and staff to take over, serving reliable stone crab claws and other shellfish tangled with pasta, good steaks. When the Cubs win the World Series, this will be the place to celebrate the occasion.

606 North Ocean Drive. (305) 923-4000. Moderate to expensive. Dinner.

GOOD PLANET CAFE
American/Fort Lauderdale

A funky high-tech setting with art gallery on the warehouse walls— described as a "Downtown Neo-Hippy Gourmet Diner" by owner Jonathan Good, who patterned this place after his sister's Silver City Cafe in New Mexico. That's where he learned to prepare everything from scratch (so don't be in a hurry here or come too late to gulp and go before a performance at the nearby Broward Center for the Performing Arts). That means "New World cuisine featuring authentic New Mexican green red chile," but it's really New Mexican and Old Italian with some Szechuan seasonings and pseudo-Greek salads added for good effect. We like the beef-free burgers served with salsa and guacamole, reubens made with turkey pastrami, and the Last Ditch Pollo Verde—the house dish in Silver City, consisting of chunks of chicken breast braced by diced green chile mingled with tomato in a cream sauce over fettuccine.

214 Southwest Second Street. (305) 527-GOOD. Inexpensive to moderate. Lunch and dinner.

Best Cuban – Broward

Put on the *ropa vieja* at Padrino's, 2500 East Hallandale Beach Boulevard, Hallandale and 801 South University Drive, Plantation.

GRAINARY CAFE
Healthfood/Deerfield Beach

Here is the place for vegetarian and macrobiotic cuisine of a fairly high order. They specialize in low fat organically-grown foods free of sugar and cholesterol—tofu lasagna, fresh grilled fish, veggie-stuffed dumplings, organically grown brown rice. No meat, no dairy, no eggs, no caffeine, but super-generous portions and they pour reverse osmosis purified water. A natural choice.

Palm Plaza, 847 South Federal Highway. (305) 360-0824. Moderate. Lunch and dinner.

GRAMPA'S BAKERY AND RESTAURANT
American/Dania

I don't know if he has any grandchildren, but Ron Grampa very definitely has a bakery. And it's a good one, with great crusty rolls that are such a relief after all the microwaved-into-mush pre-fab offerings too many restaurants rely on. The rye and whole wheat bread are also excellent, and we like them wrapped around chicken and tuna salads at noontime. In the mornings we have the corned beef hash and in the evenings, the special roast or sauteed chicken, lamb shank, the kind of stew the Hungarians call gulyas.

17 Southwest 1st Street. (305) 923-2163. Inexpensive to moderate. Breakfast, lunch and dinner.

HEMMINGWAY
American/Hollywood

The history here has nothing to do with the writer who only had one "m" in his name, but with the town—it was built as the Hollywood City Hall and was blessed with another rebirth when the French-Canadian team of perfectionists, Marie and Kerry from Kerry's restaurant on Federal, took it over in 1992, cleaning and restoring. The setting is modified Miami Beach Baroque with giant murals, satyrs and nymphs and nudes, but the menu is fairly standard stuff with prime rib, broiled trout almondine, turkey cordon bleu, orange roughy, ribeye steaks.

219 North 21st Avenue. (305) 926-5644. Moderate to expensive. Lunch and dinner.

HIGGY'S GOAL LINE CAFE
American/Sunrise

Higgy is none other than Mark Higgs, the most recent of the Miami Dolphins to become a celebrateur. The running-back signed up in '93, joining teammates Dan Marino and John Offerdahl, lending his name to a hands-on video-games- sports TV bar spread in a space that has seen many struggling failures—kind of a restaurant du jour. The menu is snack stuff and there are a few items worthy of a low-cal, low-fat training table.

Sunset Mall, 2079 North University Drive. (305) 749-3696. Inexpensive to moderate. Lunch and dinner.

HOLLY'S
American/Fort Lauderdale

For downtown breakfasts starting at 7 a.m. and lunches lasting to 4 p.m., this ground floor spread of bustling informality is the place. There's nothing fancy about the food—or the prices—but the staff is friendly and efficient and we like the sandwiches, salads and soups.

121 East Broward Boulevard. (305) 764-4227. Inexpensive. Breakfast and lunch.

HOUSE OF INDIA
Indian/Fort Lauderdale

The first House of India was established years ago on Merrick Way in Coral Gables where it was the only curried action in town. Now there are close to a dozen Indian restaurants on the Gold Coast. This is one of the least pretentious, in setting and service, but it's a reliable place to be introduced to the special breads and rice, the appetizer cakes called samosas, and some of the curries. A word of warning: unless you have asbestos for a palate stay away from vindaloo!

3060 North Andrews Avenue. (305) 566-5666. Inexpensive to moderate. Lunch and dinner.

HOUSTON'S ★★★
American/Fort Lauderdale

Imagine what it does to a manager to have his name on a brass plate at the entrance. Or to have a staff that is so well supervised and motivated that they greet newcomers and clear tables in well under a minute. There are other obvious manifestations of the fine art of running a restaurant—fresh-brewed soups, great salads, fresh fish filleted in-house, burgers and steaks grilled on hickory, roast chicken and black beans. The bar, which pours only name brands, is another study in perfection.

1451 North Federal Highway. (305) 563-2226. Moderate. Lunch and dinner.

HUNKY DORY'S
Seafood/Hollywood

Believe it or not, there actually is a Dory. It's the name of the family responsible for this Waterway hugger with its outside lineup of picnic tables, its inside bar and lounge with a lively bunch of musicians, and a menu that features seafood. Miamians make the trip here, by boat and car, just for the fresh fillets of snapper, grouper, dolphin, swordfish and tuna. We come for the wonderfully casual spirit and setting and the conch fritters, as well as the grilled fish.

1318 North Ocean Drive. (305) 925-1011. Inexpensive to moderate. Dinner.

IL GIARDINO
Italian/Fort Lauderdale

Omnipresent owners Michael and Pat Creighton were smart enough to hire executive chef Larry Lombardo and create a cheerfully sophisticated retreat. Noontime we usually have the lightly dusted broiled sole or the pasta combination of the day, and at night we start with crab cakes freckled with corn kernels and peppered with jalapenos then heightened mightily with garlic herb butter. That's followed by swordfish with a terrific Dijonaise sauce with its own boosters of cognac and green peppercorns.

609 East Las Olas Boulevard. (305) 763-3373. Moderate to expensive. Lunch and dinner.

IL PORCINO ★★★
Italian/Coral Springs

One of the smallest, most modest restaurants in the book, started in 1988 by a trio of galley veterans from Costa Cruise Lines, Filippo Ascione and the Balzano brothers, Rino and Luciano. Almost overnight they established themselves as very serious contenders for a spot on the Italian summit serving porcini-loaded risotto, butterflied baby salmon sauteed in a sage-enhanced cream sauce, red snapper in a sauce of diced plum tomatoes, black olives and onions, basil and capers; veal with gorgonzola sauce; osso buco; chicken breasts sauteed with porcini in a creamy brown sauce splashed with enough wine to give it a refined boost. Rino split off to start Il Tartufo, but this place is still a real winner.

8037 West Sample Road. (305) 344-9446. Moderate to expensive. Lunch and dinner.

IL TARTUFO ★★★★
Italian/Fort Lauderdale

Chef-owner Rino Balzano is the quiet and kindly commander and at his side is his wife Nadine, a Scot who's responsible for the decor with its Art Deco overtones and sophisticated sense of understatement. Rino's responsible for his wood-burning oven, a Tuscan revelation for Genoese Rino, and he's overwhelmed by the reduction in time for his preparation of seafood, fowl and meats. Order whatever it is he wants to commit to the high intensity heat, but first take a tour of the appetizer table to select the starters and remember to save room for something sinful from the dessert cart, saving a bit of wine from an excellent Italian list to toast the talent, and the success, of this attractive couple.

2980 North Federal Highway. (305) 564-0607. Expensive. Dinner.

JACK'S OLD FASHION HAMBURGER HOUSE
American/Oakland Park

The name says it all. This is the place to get hamburgers, excellent hamburgers, from 10:30 in the morning to 9:30 at night, seven days a week. Grilled to order and with a do-it-yourself counter for the toppings—without a plastic packet in sight.

4201 North Federal Highway. (305) 565-9960. Inexpensive. Lunch and dinner.

JAKE'S PLACE
American/Fort Lauderdale

The owners of the Floridian at 1410 East Las Olas opened this snappy little cafe to capture more of the boulevard business—all those who like solid food without the frills or fancies. The sandwiches are real mouth-benders, the salads real eye-poppers, and the burgers are real beauts. We like the half pound Ultimate Burger loaded with everything.

200 East Las Olas Boulevard. (305) 764-0200. Inexpensive. Lunch and dinner.

JAPANESE VILLAGE
Japanese/Fort Lauderdale

Chef-owner Gotaro settled this village in 1988, in the heart of a boulevard with a grand and glorious array of ethnic eats. Sit at the bar and watch Gotaro at work, expertly slicing the raw slabs of impeccably fresh fish and with the talented hands of a ceramicist, carefully but speedily molding the rice into attractive rolls named California and Las Olas. Or sit at one of the starkly furnished tables and have the sushi and sashimi delivered as prelude to sukiyaki, yosenabe, chicken and beef teriyaki, a combo of shrimp and vegetables, or steak and lobster.

716 East Las Olas Boulevard. 763-8163. Inexpensive to moderate. Lunch and dinner.

JASMINE
Thai/Margate

In addition to all the treats from the Thai kitchen, there are several Chinese offerings in this nicely appointed, happily-run hideaway. The Thai owners have trouble attracting the locals to take a dare and try something different, so they load up the early bird menu with the likes of won-ton, chow mein, sweet and sour chicken. We come for the masaman curried chicken made with cream of coconut, and the sea scallops stir-fried with onions, peppers, mushrooms, scallions and homemade chili sauce.

5279 Coconut Creek Parkway. (305) 979-5530. Inexpensive to moderate. Lunch and dinner.

JAXSON'S
American/Dania

Owner-operator Monroe Udell has been warehousing early American nostalgia here ever since he opened in 1956, dusting and polishing it occasionally, in between supervising the churning of the ice cream—35 flavors—and preparation of simple snacks, sandwiches, burgers, hot dogs. We come for the ice cream—at any time of the day.

128 South Federal Highway. (305) 923-4445. Inexpensive. Lunch and dinner.

JOE'S 17TH STREET DINER
American/Fort Lauderdale

The diner craze is still dotting the landscape with nostalgia-laden memory banks, but few of them are as extensive as this 24-hour feeder convenient to Convention Center and Port Everglades. It's had a couple of incarnations since first opening as a ripoff of Ed Debevic's in Chicago, but is now settled down to doing what diners are supposed to—serve solid, family style food at pocket-pleasing prices.

1717 Eisenhower Boulevard. (305) 527-5637. Inexpensive. Breakfast, lunch and dinner.

KELLY'S LANDING
Seafood/Fort Lauderdale

The wearing of this green originated in the Auld Sod of Massachusetts, and Boston baked beans, baked stuffed scrod, New England steamers and clam chowder, and of course Maine lobster, play a major role in the menu. They even do a Saturday night special, steak-n-beans served with brown bread. Other reasons for finding this place are the fried clams, stuffed quahogs, scallop and shrimp scampi, and the excellent half-pound burgers and half-pound sandwiches, the 35 imported beers, plus 14 from stateside breweries.

Southport Shopping Center, 1305 Southeast 17th Street.(305) 760-7009. Moderate. Lunch and dinner.

THE KING'S HEAD
British/Dania

You can't miss this marvelous pub driving to or from the beach—just look for the largest Union Jack on the road. It points the way to a quintessential pub, complete with dart board, English papers, English soccer on Sundays and Guiness, Bass Ale, Harp Lager on tap. The dining room with its grand portrait of Henry VIII on a library wall is separate from the bar. It's where partner-chef Michel Courtine, a Swiss, brings his own expertise to play in the shepherd's cottage pie, or those made with chicken, steak, kidneys and mushrooms; the fish n' chips and other typical pub grub. But he also prepares angel hair with pesto sauce, roast pork loin in a port-mushroom sauce, braised lamb shanks, tournedos in a brandy spiked cream sauce and curried chicken.

500 East Dania Beach Boulevard. (305) 922-5722. Moderate. Lunch and dinner.

LA BONNE AUBERGE   ★★★
Continental/Fort Lauderdale

This indeed is a Good Inn, the handsomely dressed domain of Michel and Juana Mouly and a friendly, professional staff proud to serve the products of chef Michel's kitchen. They're cross-cultural, trans-continental in scope, starting with the made-out-back, coarse-grained country pate and cheese-filled ravioli with a pesto sauce worthy of Genoa, lobster bisque, onion soup, quiche Lorraine, smoked Norwegian salmon and escargots Bourguignon. Among the mains we can recommend with enthusiasm are the linguine primavera, the seafood medley of scallops, shrimp, tuna and onions on a bed of angel hair, the frog legs served with pea pods, haricots vert and turnip mash; the fat-free, flavorful roast duck in a fine raspberry sauce and the Poulet Roti Bonne Auberge, the slow-roasted (50 minutes so order in advance) bird served with mushrooms and potatoes. Good wine list.

4300 North Federal Highway. (305) 776-1668. Moderate to expensive. Lunch and dinner. Closed July—August.

LA BONNE CREPE
French/Fort Lauderdale

Remember the crepe craze? The fascination with those thin-thin pancakes from Brittany? They're still found here. 33 savories and 15 sweets folded into made-to-order, oversize pancakes. The Morins, Christiane and Pierre, have been turning them out at this location since 1980, adding excellent brewed-fresh soups to the inventory along with different cakes and tarts. In a setting that always reminds us of any number of small cafes in Paris.

815 East Las Olas Boulevard. (305) 761-1515. Inexpensive. Lunch, dinner and Sunday brunch.

LA BROCHETTE
Continental/Cooper City

Chef-owner Aboud Kobaitri could have called his restaurant Shish Kabob or maybe Souvlaki—they all mean a small spit for fixing meat on the main spit and skewered meat, fish, fowl are what Aboud has been preparing ever since he opened in early 1993 after a stint at Lauderdale's La Reserve among other places. Skewer grilling is a technique derided by many, including Julia Child, who correctly comments that it's difficult to bring so many different textures and types of food to the proper state of doneness when they're all jammed together over a grill. But Aboud has obviously mastered the technique. If you want non-skewered items order calves liver, a steak, veal or fillets of fish—they're all imaginatively served and tastefully treated by Aboud, who is obviously a first class saucier. He is also serving excellent breads, butters, salads and desserts.

Embassy Lakes Shopping Center, 2635 North Hiatus Road. (305) 435-9090. Moderate to expensive. Dinner.

Best Caesar Salad

Brutus could not best the beauty assembled at Le Dome, 333 Sunset Drive, Fort Lauderdale.

LA COQUILLE ★★★
French/Fort Lauderdale

Scallops, as the name indicates, are indeed a main attraction in French chef-owner Jean Bert's 40-seat surprise, and we usually wind up ordering coquille St. Jacques for starters, when we have the strength to pass up the shrimp-filled ravioli, seafood pate and morels bathed in a rich cream sauce and placed in puff pastry. The duckling in lingonberry sauce is an interesting departure from the usual, and we also like Bert's veal chop and his handling of fresh Florida snapper and pompano, one kissed with champagne, the other with white wine.

815 East Sunrise Boulevard. (305) 467-3030. Expensive. Lunch and dinner.

LA FERME ★★★★
French/Fort Lauderdale

One of the most successful husband-wife teams in town is in residence here. While chef-owner Henri Terrier whisks away in the kitchen, Marie-Paule charms and controls the front room, demonstrating again and again that she is the sparkling personification of the perfect hostess. The setting is a long way in style from the rustic farm, La Ferme, they started with back in the 1970s. But Lyon native Henri continues to do his thing, in the same reliable way, turning out excellent veal and seafood creations, climaxed by an impossible-to-resist dessert cart. And he continues to experiment a bit, most recently figuring out how to prepare skate, a delicate surprise.

1601 East Sunrise Boulevard. (305) 764-0987. Expensive. Dinner. Closed mid-June through mid-September.

LA PERGOLA
Italian/Hollywood

True to its name, this is an arbor setting, with dangling plastic grapes everywhere, reminiscent of any number of places in the Italian countryside where we discover fine wines, fine food, fine people—under the pergola. Here we start with some pasta or the mussels marinara and then order the veal Milanese, chicken Francese or trout almondine wh*'* enjoying the piano music.

939 North Federal Highway. (305) 927-0405. Moderate.

LA PERLA
Italian/Fort Lauderdale

We love the name. This is a pearl, polished to a brilliant sheen by Vincent de Leo, "Vincenzo", front man extraordinaire, who has a kitchen with comparable talent. Among other headliners we like the snail starter, Lumache al Funghetto, a bunch of them with mushrooms in a superlatively rich dark sauce reeking of the inner forest. We also find good cause to praise the handling of salmon and swordfish carpaccio, the risotto zapped with the special snap of Trevisana radicchio and the osso buco. Excellent Italian wine selection.

1818 East Sunrise Boulevard. (305) 765-1950. Expensive. Dinner.

LA PIAZZA
Italian/Fort Lauderdale

The setting in this bistro-brasserie-cafe-trattoria is sensational, with colors of the Italian flag painted everywhere, with umbrellas, opera posters, and imported wares—it's an Italian street fair. With lotsa pizza, pasta and such satisfiers as the golden brown crispy Calamari di Giuseppone and pork chops laden with rosemary. The soups are fresh-brewed and beautiful and the family style serving of salad is a real knockout.

Stirling Square, 2901 Stirling Road. (305) 985-1027. Moderate. Lunch and dinner.

LA RESERVE
French/Fort Lauderdale

Guy and Richard Teboul, natives of northern France, have assembled one of the best cellars in Florida— some 225 labels, including close to 50 California cabs and a scattering of museum bottlings priced in the stratosphere. They make it all available in a stunningly romantic room on the shore of the Intracoastal, and use it to advantage to complement the outpourings of their French kitchen: frog legs in garlic butter, Florida lobster au gratin, snapper Deauville and chateaubriand.

3115 Northeast 32nd Avenue. (305) 563-6644. Expensive. Dinner.

LA STELLA ★★
Italian/Sunrise

There are many simple little pizzerias and would-be trattorias in West Broward, and a few feederies with enough class to be categorized as ristorantes like this star, a family-friendly spot with a staff that shows care and concern and with a kitchen that turns out far better than average pasta and veal dishes. The shrimp Francese is a particular favorite of ours. Select wine list.

Spring Tree Club Shopping Center, 3801 North University Drive. (305) 748-4788. Moderate to expensive. Dinner.

LA TAVERNETTA ★★
Italian/Tamarac

Carole and G.G. Romano hold forth in this trattoria tribute to all things Italian, with the red, white and green everywhere, along with hanging garlics and peppers and mementos of hometown Ischia, that resort island between the bays of Gaeta and Naples—noted for its flavorful fruits and vegetables. G.G. is best known for his shrimp creations, his chicken primavera, eggplant rollatine, and clams casino.

8455 West McNab Road. (305) 722-1831. Moderate to expensive. Dinner.

LA TRAVIATA ★★★
Italian/Fort Lauderdale

What is arguably the most popular opera of all time is here immortalized with giant paintings of tragic heroine Violetta. But the only diva in the place is the "Antipasto del Soprano" as assembled by chef-owner Sergio Teruggi, who also has a chicken creation named "Sovrano Loren," veal scallops covered with a suggestion of eggplant and baked with mozzarella in a creamy tomato sauce. Maitre d'-partner Joe Corteo does sing, but not Limbiamo ne'lieti calici— Let us quaff from the wine cup overflowing.

2104 East Oakland Park Boulevard. (305) 564-7720. Expensive. Dinner.

LA VERANDA
Italian/Pompano Beach

A total rehab and expansion of this tribute to the talents and hard work of Franco and Gianpiero took place in 1990 and it's a treat to watch them work the floor, guiding their guests through the specials of the night and choosing the right wines. It's all reminiscent of something special in Tuscany, and at Christmas time few restaurants can compete with their decorations and festive spirits.

2121 East Atlantic Boulevard. (305) 943-7390. Moderate. Dinner.

LARRY'S ★
Seafood/Fort Lauderdale

Since the Bicentennial Year of 1976 Guy Larielle has been the Larry of this comfortable, cheerful raw bar with a lot of repeat customers and a pocketbook-pleasing menu. We start here with the freshly shucked little necks or the steamed oysters and then sail into the broiled seafood platter, Cathy's Spanish stew of seafood served with garlic bread, or the scallops and shrimps simmered in garlic butter with broccoli, green peppers, onions and a splash of white wine. As a sure sign of success, there was a major expansion and redecoration in 1993 but it did not destroy the casual, informal feel of the place.

5770 North Federal Highway. (305) 776-6170. Inexpensive to moderate. Lunch and dinner.

LAS OLAS CAFE
Continental/Fort Lauderdale

In the right season, lunching and dining in the sheltered courtyard just a few feet from the boulevard is a delightful getaway experience, but when the heat and humidity take over we happily retreat to the tiny inside dining room. Either place, it's the chef that counts most here, the chef with the imagination to stuff jumbo shrimp with mozzarella and wrap them with prosciutto, to coat a generous fillet of fresh snapper with sauteed red onions, or present it on a bed of spinach with toasted pine nuts.

922 East Las Olas Boulevard. (305) 524-4300. Expensive. Lunch and dinner.

LAS PALMAS ★
Spanish-Cuban/Margate

When Castro seized power in 1960 the Cubans started coming to South Florida in force, and soon there were isolated clumps of Cubans north of Miami's little Havana, including the crew that established this reliable provider of so many good things Cuban style—the chopped beef and shrimp in Creole sauces, the shredded beef called "old clothes," ropa vieja, the integrated black bean and white rice blend known as the Moors and the Christians, the fried plantains, garlic-loaded yuca and the creamy pudding called flan.

998 South State Road 7. (305) 973-5978. Inexpensive to moderate. Lunch and dinner.

Best Mexican Restaurant – South Florida

The Pria brothers do it all at San Angel, 2822 East Commercial Boulevard. Fort Lauderdale.

LAS VEGAS I, II, III
Cuban/Hollywood/Plantation/Lighthouse Point

I and II have been pleasing patrons in Hollywood and Plantation since the mid-1970s, and making enough money to finance Las Vegas III, largest by far of the trio, but serving the same kind of top quality food, budget-pleasing plates and platters filled with sweet plantains, white rice and black beans, chicken and yellow rice, shrimp creole; fried, grilled and roast pork, and fantastic flan plus something sensational called three milk cake.

Las Vegas I, 1212 North State Road, Hollywood, (305) 961-1001; Las Vegas II, 7015 West Broward Boulevard, Plantation, (305) 584-4400; Las Vegas III, 4000 North Federal Highway, Lighthouse Point, (305) 783-5338. Inexpensive to moderate. Lunch and dinner.

L'AVENTURE
French/Pompano Beach

A tres, tres charming doll house that is always cheerful, always eager to greet the guests with Georgette out front and husband Desire in the kitchen. You'll meet him as you walk through the kitchen from the parking lot. In place since 1983, these natives of Brittany had extensive experience in top-of-the-line Manhattan restaurants before seeking their place in the sun. Among the Gallic headliners we like are the red snapper and salmon in creamy dill sauce, shrimp sauteed with sherry, butter and garlic; liver and onions, and Desire's own version of bouillabaisse.

3332 East Atlantic Boulevard. (305) 941-1724. Moderate. Dinner. Closed month of September.

LE BISTRO ★
French/Fort Lauderdale

What a charming place chef Alain and his wife Pamela have created, filling a single, small room with lots of lace on the windows and tabletops, adding an art gallery and enough artifacts to transport guests somewhere far away from Federal Highway. The menu works its own magic—for the pocket as well as the palate with budget-stretching fixed price meals and blackboard specials, simply, honestly prepared without haute cuisine ruffles and flourishes. We like the angel hair pomodoro, the pair of veal chops, the trout meuniere with an almond shower on top.

4626 North Federal Highway, (305) 946-9240. Inexpensive to moderate. Dinner.

Best Wine Lists

Oenophilic fantasies are fulfilled at Fort Lauderdale's Chameleon and Down Under and Boca Raton's La Vieille Maison.

LE DOME ★★★
American/Fort Lauderdale

Under the aegis of veteran restaurateur Doug Mackle, Le Dome has returned to the summit, serving food and wines worthy of the setting and the panorama views. Chef Johnny Kromann joined the family in 1993 and is producing a grand array of the classic continental specialties with New Wave twists and treats. For starters there's gravlaks paired with house-smoked salmon served in Dijon aioli sauce; a beautiful bisque boosted with chunks of Maine lobster, and their justifiably famous Caesar. Entrees include a slow-roasted rack of lamb, covered with bread-crumbs flavored with herbs of Provence held in place by Dijon, and served with chasseur sauce and cream cheese polenta; roast Hudson Valley duck; chargrilled California pork tenderloin marinated with garlic and glazed with honey, and a signature dish, swordfish given the King Oscar salute, not with sardines, but with fresh asparagus and lobster with sauce bearnaise. The wine list is in the capable hands of Master Sommelier Mark Spivak—take his suggestions seriously and get on his newsletter mailing list.

333 Sunset Drive. (305) 463-3303. Expensive. Dinner.

LE VAL DE LOIRE ★
Continental/Deerfield Beach

A native of France's Loire Valley out front and her German-born husband in the back make this place work and make them one of the most popular couples in town. Josiane and Manfred Vogt—remember the names and remember to order Manfred's incredibly good escargot, his beef bourguignon or Stroganoff, or any of the medallions of veal given the special salutes of Francaise, marsala or parmesan. But save space for something sinful from his collection of high cal desserts.

1576 Southeast 3rd Court. (305) 427-5354. Moderate. Lunch and dinner.

THE LEFT BANK ★★★
French/Fort Lauderdale

Jean-Pierre Brehier is not one to rest on laurels. A few years ago, he started a wine store around the corner, and when that closed he worked hard to double the size of his restaurant. Then came his glossy newsletter and his own television cooking show. But all the while he's supervising and cheffing, producing such headliners as snapper in a champagne mustard sauce, chicken with three peppers and flash of brandy, veal scallops with baby shrimp in a pesto-mushroom butter sauce, and filet mignon with a bourbon-pistachio sendoff.

214 Southeast 6th Avenue. (305) 462-5376. Expensive. Dinner.

LEO'S SALTY SEA
Seafood/Deerfield Beach

New Yorkers might remember Leo Tejeiro's Salty Sea at 108 East 60th Street. Like so many restaurateurs he fled south, finding his own place in the sun, furnishing his corner storefront with all kinds of nautical memorabilia, attracting a bar crowd and those who come for his excellent luncheon burgers and french fries, and again at night for the black bean soup and fillets of fish.

1136 East Hillsboro Boulevard. (305) 421-3925. Inexpensive to moderate. Lunch and dinner. Closed mid-June to mid-September.

LESTER'S DINER
American/Fort Lauderdale

Diners are all the rage now, but not too many years ago Lester's was the only game in town and they're still doing what they did then to fill the stools and booths—serving low-cost food without any of the pizazz of the new guys on the block, lots of pies and cakes, blue-plate specials and the 14-ounce cup of coffee—their hallmark.

250 State Road 84, Fort Lauderdale, (305) 525-5641; 4701 Coconut Creek Parkway, Margate, (305) 979-4722. Inexpensive. Breakfast, lunch and dinner.

L'HOSTERIA
Italian/Tamarac

Family operation with a lot of personal attention by a staff obviously eager to make their way in the local restaurant jungle, and to please the legions of loyal fans who come back night after night. Why not? The clams oreganata are sensational, the pasta treated respectfully when the sauces are added, the filet mignon grilled to perfection and the signature veal scallops are super, garnished with artichoke hearts and mushrooms in lemon butter. We also like their wine list.

Tamarac Shopping Plaza, 6646 Northeast 57th Street. (305) 722-0340. Moderate to expensive. Dinner. Closed August through mid-September.

L'ILE DE FRANCE ★★★
French/Fort Lauderdale

In 1991 Sandra and Remi Coulon took over this landmark, originally the first creperie in Florida, and stamped their own personalities on the place, experimenting with hot stones on the table for fat free, do-it-yourself cooking. A native of Burgundy who came straight off the yacht of the Aga Khan, chef Remi has a sure hand assembling the hazelnut-freckled duck pate, calf's liver with a balsamic-roasted garlic sauce, poached sole with champagne-ginger, and scallops of veal with a honey-sweetened mustard. His tarte tatin is terrific. The fixed price menus make this a good-value-for-the-money stop on the budget trail.

3025 North Ocean Boulevard. (305) 565-9006. Moderate. Lunch and dinner.

Best Poolside Bar

Dive into the watering hole at Bahia Cabana Beach Resort, 3001 Harbor Drive, Fort Lauderdale.

MAI-KAI ★★
Polynesian/Fort Lauderdale

The only other year-round Polynesian show in Florida is up Disney Way, and they're a newcomer, compared to this longest-running nightclub revue in the state. The flame-throwers and sword-swingers are exciting to watch, and so too the Mai-Kai girls, elaborately costumed. Also eye-popping are the Molokai bar and authentic South Seas furnishings all about. Since 1956 this dramatically designed tourist attraction has been packing 'em in, serving a variety of starters and entrees that are generally categorized into what Trader Vic (or was it Don the Beachcomber?) called Polynesian. Skip the appetizers and concentrate on the goodies from the Chinese wood-burning ovens.

3599 North Federal Highway. (305) 563-3272. Expensive. Dinner.

MAMA MIA ITALIAN RISTORANTE
Italian/Hollywood

An outside-inside setting without ever going outside—umbrella-shaded tables and a profusion of plants do the trick. A family-pleasing big spread spot with a smiling, speedy team bringing the kind of American-Italian food we've all found we can't live without—fried calamari and calzones, sausage and peppers, eggplant parmesan and cheesecake, served in generous portions. At lunchtime we like the Italian subs.

1818 South Young Circle. (305) 923-0555. Moderate. Lunch and dinner.

MANERO'S
American/Hallandale

Here's a real blast from the hallowed halls of golfdom past, with a red meat approach to sustenance noon and night. Start your retro trip with a session in the 19th Hole filled with marvelous memory-joggers and be sure to order the gorgonzola thunderstorm for your bottomless salad bowl, the onion rings, lightly breaded and deep-fried, and of course a steak. Who's counting calories and cholesterol?

2600 East Hallandale Beach Boulevard. (305) 456-1100. Moderate to expensive. Lunch and dinner.

MANGO'S ★★
American/Fort Lauderdale

John Day, singer and restaurateur, already responsible for Coconuts on the Waterway, opened this sidewalk cafe on the street of streets in 1993, immediately starting a trend and enlivening the boulevard of unbroken dreams tremendously. We like to sit outside, munching on a thickly-packed sandwich or twirling the Garlic Lover's Pasta, working over a charcoal-grilled filet mignon bearnaise, some chicken puff pie, slow-baked grouper with citrus sauce, or a heartsmart New Wave Salad of veggies and fusili dressed with basil vinaigrette. Start with the fish dip and finish with the chocoholics climax, an awesome artery-clogger of a double fudge brownie with chocolate sauce and Haagen-Dazs ice cream. Live entertainment at night.

904 East Las Olas Boulevard. (305) 523-5001. Moderate. Lunch and dinner.

MARCELLO ITALIAN RESTAURANT
Italian/Hollywood

Overshadowed in size by the neighboring Mama Mia whose menu is as flashy and as encyclopedic as Marcello's is modest, this cozy and comfortable little trattoria complete with red checked tablecloths, overhead wine racks and espresso machine, offers solid, freshly prepared food including good eggplant and veal parmesan, spicy chicken scarpariello, and lots of garlic.

1822 South Young Circle. (305) 923-1055. Moderate. Lunch and dinner.

MARCELLO RISTORANTE ★
Italian/Deerfield Beach

I'm not sure if Marcello-Deerfield or Marcello-Hollywood came first, but there is no relation and the slight name difference is apparently legal enough to allow two in the county. This is indeed a ristorante, and the feeling is formal in a friendly way. We like the starters of clams casino and oreganata, the angel hair mingled with a simple plum tomato-basil-garlic sauce, the veal Francese and the servings of snapper and salmon.

718 South Federal Highway. (305) 427-4909. Moderate to expensive. Dinner.

MARIO THE BAKER
Italian/Sunrise

If you're looking for the ultimate garlic roll, this is the place. Mario is a master at making them and built such a reputation and a following that he could modernize, expand and come up with this neatly appointed highway roadhouse. Here he does much more than garlic rolls and great cheesecake; he churns out all kinds of pasta and eggplant parmesan, chicken cacciatore, veal marsala, shrimp Francese.

2220 University Drive. (305) 742-3333. Moderate. Lunch and dinner.

MARTHA'S
American/Hollywood

A split personality kind of place with a second deck for boaters and others who want to stay casual, and a ground floor of considerable elegance—not really what one expects to find in this location a few hundred conch shells south of the bridge. The table appointments have quality linens, china, glass and flatware; the staff tries hard to be formal and knowledgeable; and the kitchen turns out reliable fillets of fish with interesting sauces, good steaks and some pasta.

6024 North Ocean Drive. (305) 923-5444. Moderate to expensive. Lunch and dinner.

McDIVOT'S
American/Margate

This is a country club with a lot of pizzazz and golf memorabilia everywhere. We like the beautifully landscaped grounds, the Southern Plantation look of the building, the tightly supervised staff which moves with unusual efficiency and promptness. And we like the carefully executed menu with such specialties as broiled sole mornay on a bed of spinach, almond coated shrimp and intoxicated pork—marinated in spiced red wine.

Carolina Club, 3011 Rock Island Road, Margate. (305) 753-3500. Moderate. Lunch and dinner.

MEJICO GRANDE
Mexican/Davie

Family oriented pleasant place with red colors all about, comfortable booths and a menu bristling with such Especialidades de la Casa as Chili Davie, made from beef tenderloin and served with refried beans, sour cream, jalapeno slices and cheese for rolling into flour tortillas. The shrimp and crab nachos are also worth the trip.

Lincoln Park Shopping Plaza, 6890 Stirling Road. (305) 963-1205. Inexpensive. Lunch and dinner.

MICHAEL ANTHONY'S
Italian/Fort Lauderdale

This tiny, single storefront was opened in January 1991, by Michael, formerly a chef at the Boca Raton Resort and Club, and his wife, Lisa, who handles the front room. The competition can be crushing but Mike does some good things in addition to the usual—lobster Portofino which translates to a saute with fresh spinach and freshly made marinara, and a shrimp-mushroom melange in a lemon-butter sauce, plus a lot of specials predicated on market supply.

Cuningham Plaza, 3343 East Oakland Park Boulevard. (305) 568-2224. Moderate to expensive. Dinner.

MICHAEL'S
Italian/Fort Lauderdale

With a father out in the kitchen running the show, a son in charge of the front room, and a mother quietly overseeing both of them, this is an undiscovered Italian Ristorante, overlooked by too many diners lost in the forest of competitors. The classics of the American-Italian culinary repertoire are done with finesse, and the shrimp filled with bacon and spinach is marvelous. We also like the formality of the room, the table appointments, the intimate ambiance.

1635 North Federal Highway. (305) 566-2690. Moderate. Dinner.

MIKE'S CLAM BAR
Seafood/Sunrise

What started as a modest little snackery loyal to the name is now a full scale restaurant. The bar is still intact and usually filled with a casual crowd hunkered into their half shells. We sit at table slurping the raw mollusks, gently slicing the fillets of grilled fresh fish and digging into the recesses of the Maine lobster, all the while appreciating the persistency and perseverance of Mike.

3197 North University Drive. (305) 741-2005. Moderate. Dinner.

MISTRAL
Mediterranean/Fort Lauderdale

The only other South Florida Mistral—the cold northwest wind that blows across southern France—was in Key West years ago, and was strictly French. This little sidewalk-straddling, indoor-outdoor cafe, opened in July 1993 by the same team responsible for Sage, the Fort Lauderdale French-American cafe, is an entirely different kind of operation. The new venture is on the oceanfront, a happy presence along the recently reborn A1A. It's the hopeful harbinger of more cafes to come as Fort Lauderdale beach, FoBe, tries to follow the lead of South Miami Beach, SoBe. The food is almost a secondary consideration in this trailblazer with its nightly live jazz, but there's promise in the tapas appetizers, the gazpacho variation—grilled shrimp and steak, and the kind of designer pizzas found all over SoBe.

201 State Road A1A. (305) 463-4900. Moderate. Lunch and dinner.

MOMBASA BAY
Caribbean/Fort Lauderdale

If you're wondering where it is, don't look on the African coast; look at the shore of the Intracoastal near Shooters; look and listen—for the nightly reggae—while downing conch chowder and fritters, one of the several burgers, a seafoodsalad, some grilled shrimp, complementing it with one of 30 imported beers or a great tropical drink. A fun place and a great location. Our hats are off to owners Amos Chess and Ray Shamouelian who brought Mombasa to our shores in the summer of 1990.

3051 Northeast 32nd Avenue. (305) 565-7441. Moderate. Lunch and dinner.

MONTEGO GRILL AND LOUNGE
Jamaican/Lauderhill

Hey Mon! Here's the place for ackee and salt cod, curried goat, jerk pork, sour sop, red beans and rice oozing with coconut milk and, of course, Johnny cakes. The setting is not exactly a resort hotel on Montego Bay, but it's vintage—and friendly.

4077 Northwest 16th Street. (305) 733-7223. Inexpensive. Lunch and dinner.

NAM LONG
Vietnamese/Lauderdale Lakes

In 1993 this strip mall storefront, opened three years earlier, doubled its size, so it must be doing something right. We confirm that fact every time we spoon into one of their superlative soups, the kind where the diner adds the bean sprouts, leaf lettuce and sprigs of mint—to maximize crunch and freshness of flavor. You do the same when adding the sauce to the delicate Banh Beo, the soft rice cakes. The sauce is described as Nam Long Special Sauce, but it's really Nuoc Mam, the basic Vietnamese fish blend made by putting alternate layers, seven in all, of salt and leftover fish parts in a container and pouring water over it. The owners and chefs here are from Saigon and they reflect beautifully the culinary traditions of the south. It's the best Vietnamese restaurant in the county.

4461 North State Road 7. (305) 485-6079. Inexpensive. Lunch and dinner.

Best Bread – Belgian – French

The staff of life at the homey French Place, 360 East McNab Road, Pompano Beach.

NAMI
Japanese/Pembroke Pines

Since 1988 this outpost of sushi and sukiyaki has been holding the fort in a modern strip mall, providing an oasis of tranquility from the highway and hustle outside. Non-stop Japanese music promotes the feeling of escape as you sit at the 12-stool sushi bar or relax at one of the glass-topped tables deciding which of the raw seafood starters to order—the full color photos are under the glass. The last time here we kicked off with cobia, baby octopus, red snapper and tuna, each impeccably fresh and artfully presented on a block of white rice, some tied with a strip of seaweed, all of it begging to be dipped into the soy sauce zapped with the green wasabi fire. Dolphin teriyaki was the next course and it was superlative, as was the peanut butter pie for dessert. Talk about cross-cultural cuisine!

8381 Pines Boulevard. (305) 432-2888. Moderate to expensive. Lunch and dinner.

NICK'S ITALIAN KITCHEN–NICK'S UPSTAIRS ★
Italian/Fort Lauderdale

Nick—otherwise known as Dominick—sold so many pizzas downstairs that he opened something far fancier on the second deck, bringing in entertainers and installing a menu with more pizazz. In a setting of brick, brass and glass, framed by above-it-all windows, Nick compiled an extensive menu—26 pastabilities, eight seafood entrees, a half dozen chicken and eggplant choices, a trio of steaks and ten veal selections, specialties of the house. We like the angel hair with a simple garlic, basil and heart of tomato sauce, or a Nick variation, adding tiny peas and bits of prosciutto. For the main action, what better test of their veal than by ordering it picante style?

3496 North Ocean Boulevard. (305) 563-6441. Inexpensive. Lunch and dinner. Open with delivery until 4 a.m.

NOBI
Japanese/Fort Lauderdale

A postage stamp cottage that was one of the first of an ever-increasing number of sushi servers in South Florida counties, this one with a counter along one wall—perfect for watching the chefs go through their paces— and booths along the other, for sitting in comfort while devouring tempura and teriyaki-treated meats, sorting through the ingredients of a bubbling sukiyaki, and having the fun of do-it-yourself shabu-shabu.

3020 North Federal Highway. (305) 561-3586. Moderate. Lunch and dinner.

OCEAN ROOM
American/Fort Lauderdale

A comfortable memory bank opened in 1965 and still preserving the decor and design of the time, right down to the keyboard vocalist at dinnertime. No cute theme here, just the ocean and beach past the wall of windows and the feeling of being thrust back into time. That sense is strengthened when you order a dinner of fried chicken with mashed potatoes (alas! not the real thing), a filet mignon, snapper or sole almondine.

Ireland's Inn, 2220 North Atlantic Boulevard. (305) 565-6661. Moderate to expensive. Breakfast, lunch and dinner.

OLD FLORIDA BAR-B-QUE
Barbecue/Oakland Park

To find this shoe box a few feet from a roaring highway, leave the windows open and follow the scent of burning hickory. We like the honesty of the ribs and chicken, the baked beans, and the friendliness of the staff. This is almost the smallest BBQ shack in the book—only Tom Jr.'s in Delray Beach is more minuscule.

1388 East Oakland Park Boulevard. (305) 561-1877. Inexpensive to moderate. Lunch and dinner.

OLD FLORIDA SEAFOOD HOUSE ★
Seafood/Wilton Manors/Sunrise

With a large raw bar by the entrance, a separate dining room with booths, and a private room in the back, separated and accented by some collectibles here and there, this is a comfortable and pleasantly served place to enjoy a seafood snack or feast. We usually start with a dozen bivalves on the half shell, move on to one of their chowders before settling into scrod which is sauteed in garlic butter, a fillet of salmon or swordfish steak. We also like the way they handle shrimp.

1414 Northeast 26th Street, Wilton Manors, (305) 566-1044; 4535 North Pine Island Road, Sunrise, (305) 572-0444. Moderate to expensive. Dinner.

OLD HEIDELBERG
German/Fort Lauderdale

Gemuetlich gasthaus close to the autobahn and authentic enough to have a Bavarian band on hand and a stream of specialities, such wunderbar winners as jager, paprika-rahm, wiener and ziguener schnitzels, liver dumpling soup, brat- and knockwurst, kielbasa and nuernberger with sauerkraut, pork shank and sauerbraten—enough to make the German food lover declare Ich hab mein herz in Heidelberg verloren—I left my heart in Heidelberg.

900 Southwest 24th Street. (305) 463-6747. Moderate to expensive. Lunch and dinner.

OLDE TOWNE CHOP HOUSE ★
American/Fort Lauderdale

A beautifully restored turn of the century tavern in the heart of historic Himarshee Village, convenient to the Center of Performing Arts. Added to those advantages is the quality of the food, the variety of the menu— medallions of venison, loin of buffalo, smoked wild boar with apricot demi-glace, steak and kidney pie, gravlaks and rainbow trout. Start a meal with the hearty steak-potato soup, proceed to a super Caesar before ordering a steak. On Wednesdays they feature meatloaf and mashed potatoes—with real potatoes and real gravy!

Himarshee Village, 301 Southwest 2nd Street. (305) 522-1253. Expensive. Lunch and dinner.

OLD SPAIN ★
Spanish-Continental/Hollywood

The name could just as well be Old Europe for the menu has been spanning the continent ever since 1990 when chef-owner Richard Wolczik-Pourtney took over from Juan Abella. Philadelphia-born Wolczik-Pourtney, graduate of Florida International University, spent a half dozen years as chef of Miami's Banker's Club and then in Dusseldorf at the Vier Jahrseiten Hotel, where he honed his skills and learned the secrets of European cooking. It all shows, whether you have the paella or chateaubriand. A guitarist plays nightly and there's a flamenco show on the weekends.

2333 Hollywood Boulevard. (305) 921-8485. Moderate to expensive. Lunch and dinner.

OLYMPIA FLAME
American/Greek/Deerfield Beach

The Katsenos clan, Gina, Tom and George, are in charge of this best diner in Broward County, open at 5:30 a.m. for the early birds, serving terrific omelets and other eye-opening staples. Later in the day are the mouth-bending sandwiches, freshly-made salads or such full-blown Greek delights as stuffed spinach leaves, spinakopita, spinach pie and mousaka—no translation needed. The staff is a lively one and very user-friendly.

80 South Federal Highway. (305) 480-8402. Inexpensive. Breakfast, lunch and dinner.

Best Baked Potato

Idahos all the way, at Runyon's, 9810 West Sample Road, Coral Springs.

OUTBACK STEAKHOUSE
American/Plantation/Coral Springs/Pembroke Pines/Fort Lauderdale

No, I'm not going to call this Australian. The only thing Down Under is the wording on the absurd menu with such Crocodile Dundee cutsies as "Jackeroo Chops," "Chicken on the Barbie," "Drover's Platter," "Botany Bay Fish of the Day," "Kookaburra Wings," and "Walkabout Soup." It's all strictly meat and potatoes American fare without a kangaroo in sight. But the prices are right, the service is well-supervised and efficient and the setting is sheer simplicity. There's a clone in Boca Raton and others all over Florida.

Jacaranda Square, 1823 B North Pine Island Road, Plantation (305) 370-9956; 650 Riverside Drive, Coral Springs, (305) 345-5965; 7841 Pines Boulevard, Pembroke Pines, (305) 981-5300; 6201 North Federal Highway, Fort Lauderdale, (305) 771-4390. Moderate. Dinner.

P. AUGUST
American/Coral Springs

The full name could be Pamela K. August. With partner Patrick Festa she started this tropically refreshing bar and grill in the 1980s, using the kitchen-on-view LA Cafe approach to design. We start our meals here with the oysters Moscow, meaning with horseradish-spiked sour cream and dabs of two caviars, then have a Caesar with grilled chicken or dolphin, followed by sauteed chicken or veal with garlic-enhanced mushrooms, roast peppers and sun-dried tomatoes; or roast duck with an apricot-mustard glaze.

10436 West Atlantic Boulevard. (305) 344-9997. Moderate to expensive. Dinner.

Best Chinese Restaurant – Broward

Rainbow Palace woks wonders in a palace of great class, 2787 East Oakland Park Boulevard, Fort Lauderdale.

PADRINO'S ★
Cuban/Hallandale/Plantation

What started as a simple little shack several miles west is now a full-blown restaurant in a modern building only a few blocks from the ocean. And, opened in 1992, Padrino's II. Both are usually packed with patrons, Latinos and gringos alike, who have come to rely on the quality—and the prices—of the Cuban classics, prepared and presented with pride, class, and a lot of friendly smiles. .

2500 East Hallandale Beach Boulevard, Hallandale, (305) 456-4550; 801 South University Drive, Plantation, (305) 476-5777. Inexpensive to moderate. Lunch and dinner.

PAESANO
Italian/Fort Lauderdale

What Mario and Maria Spinaci started as a fun trattoria in 1975 is now a twice-as-large grand ristorante complete with piano bar and a formal staff that reflects the professionalism of the owners. The specials of the day are where to concentrate your efforts but feel confident with any of the farinaceous offerings, the liver Venetian style, the veal piccata or Francese. The wines are excellent and Mario knows his cellar.

1301 East Las Olas Boulevard. (305) 467-3266. Expensive. Lunch and dinner.

PAPA GALLI'S
Italian/Pembroke Pines

An outstanding example of the new trattoria-pizzeria trend—spacious, modern, kitchen and brick oven on view, and reasonable prices for an almost endless selection of pastas, soups, salads. The weekday luncheon buffet is a real budget pleaser as are the early bird dinners which include soup, salad, good garlic rolls and dessert.

9893 Pines Boulevard. (305) 432-8300. Inexpensive. Lunch and dinner.

PASTA PASTA ★
Italian/Fort Lauderdale

The name says it all, or almost all—the soups are good too. It's heaven for dieters and everyone who wants to freak out on farinaceous fare. There's a feeding frenzy as patrons twirl, spoon and slurp the 35 pastabilities with ten different kinds of noodles, whirlies and curlicues. It's all the handiwork of owner Maria Talerico and her brothers, Lenny and Tony, in the kitchen, and nephew Andrew out front where Maria is usually to be found. Welcome to Pasta Paradise!

3042-B North Federal Highway. (305) 563-7455. Moderate. Dinner.

PELICAN PUB
Seafood/Pompano Beach

Waterfront location by the Hillsboro Inlet and specializing in seafood shack informality, spiffy service, fresh selections of dolphin, snapper, grouper and whatever else comes off the boats. We like the conch chowder, shrimp in garlic butter and broiled salmon.

2635 North Riverside Drive. (305) 785-8550. Moderate. Lunch and dinner.

PICCOLO CAFE ★
Italian/Fort Lauderdale

It's an accurate name for this minuscule storefront with 37 chairs—if they really do some squeezing. But there has to be room left for Mama Pauline Bokis to make her rounds, explaining the blackboard specials and how great the chef is, her son Billy. "We don't overdo anything, not too much garlic or too much basil, spices or peppers," she declares while describing the complimentary forcaccio, the Vitello Rosmarina, fettuccine carbonara or with gorgonzola bechamel sauce sprinkled with pine nuts, the thick swordfish steak, the Zuppa di Mare and the mussels with a fine fra diavolo compliment.

Plaza 3000, 3000 North Federal Highway. (305) 563-1395. Moderate. Dinner.

PIETRO'S
Italian/Davie

The multi-talented chef-owner, Pietro Orscahe, did all the refurbishing of this strip mall retreat—he and wife Karen. He worked a magnificent copper hunt scene sculpture into the fireplace mantle, did major carpentry and electric work, a bit of painting and touching up before getting into the kitchen where he cooks up an Italian storm. We like the stuffed artichokes, swordfish Livornese, meaning with capers but at Pietro's also with clams, mussels, a mound of linguine and a side dish of sauteed spinach. It's consumed while listening to operatic arias and toasting Pietro's achievement with one of his select Italian wines. The service is formal but not too much so—my waiter was humming along with the tenors on the tapes.

8236 Griffin Road. (305) 434-7070. Moderate to expensive. Dinner.

PINK BUDDHA
Chinese/Davie

Centerpiece of the decor in this large and well-lighted restaurant is a large Buddha—laughing. It could represent owner Raymond Ho, Hong Kong native whose New Lotus Inn for a decade was the best Chinese restaurant in Hallandale. He's now laughed his way west, overseeing a crew of chefs capable of turning out Cantonese, Hunan, Mandarin, Szechuan and Shanghai specialties and offering to cost-conscious westerners, lunch and dinner buffets.

University Creek Plaza, 5949 South University Drive. (305) 680-3388. Moderate. Lunch and dinner.

PITA PARADISE
Middle Eastern/Fort Lauderdale

Beachgoers take note! And lovers of hummus, tahini and falafel. This postage stamp a block from the beach is a great place to stuff your pita pockets, indulge handsomely in vegetarian waist-watchers and the classic sweets of the Levant.

2933 East Las Olas Boulevard. (305) 760-4727. Inexpensive. Lunch and dinner.

PLUM ROOM
Continental/Fort Lauderdale

Upstairs from Yesterday's and thankfully insulated from the noise of the adjacent disco, this is one of those restaurants that tries to be Maxim's. The service is tuxedoed formal and fussy, the colors loyal to the name, the wine list overpriced but impressive. In season they have special evenings of wild game in addition to the regular menu featuring Petaluma snails and pignolas in phyllo, bathed in garlic-beurre blanc; poached salmon Veronique, and veal loin with crab, shrimp and two sauces—bordelaise and bearnaise.

3001 East Commercial Boulevard. (305) 561-4400. Expensive. Dinner.

POMODORO
Italian/Fort Lauderdale

Milan-native Piero Manegavvi teams up with his American wife, Linda, (who owns the book shop next door), to create a unique little cafe, one with a counter from which you select whatever it is Piero has found fresh in the market, prepared with heart-smart finesse. The pizza is very good, the pasta dishes as beautiful to consume as they are to look at.

2908 East Commercial Boulevard. (305) 491-7463. Inexpensive. Lunch (in season only) and dinner. Closed August.

PONTE VECCHIO
Italian/Fort Lauderdale

Half the size of one of the smaller shops on the famous bridge, but that means the staff can concentrate its efforts to polish and perfect. And that means far better than average veal prepared a dozen different ways—we like the rack and the chops—and good seafood, shrimp fra diavolo, salmon with green peppercorns, snapper pescatore and the harvest from the deep known as zuppa di pesce.

2500 East Commercial Boulevard. (305) 772-4138. Expensive. Dinner.

Best Italian Restaurant – Broward

Rino and Nadine's magnifico Il Tartufo, 2980 North Federal Highway, Fort Lauderdale.

PRIMAVERA
Italian/Fort Lauderdale

From the eye-popping table of appetizers to the dessert cart loaded with Italian temptations this is a grand ristorante of the first rank. Sit in a position to watch the polished performance as you're gently guided through the intricacies of the night's offerings, introduced by that joyously arranged table of appetizers near the entrance—in the best Italian manner. What to order? Let captain and waiter guide you through the circles to paradise. We've never been disappointed or found the staff failing to deliver the promises spoken and observed.

830 East Oakland Park Boulevard. (305) 564-6363. Expensive. Dinner. Closed mid-August to mid-October.

PUNJAB
Indian/Fort Lauderdale

Originally in far simpler digs on Oakland Park Boulevard, this outpost of a hard-working family from Moglai in North India provides a good introduction to the uninitiated. Start with a variety tray of appetizers, and get to know the definitions of samosa, bhujia, pakora and papadum; and then charge into another assortment—chicken, lamb, shrimp cooked in the charcoal-charged clay tandoor oven and treated to all kinds of spices and marinades.

5975 North Federal Highway. (305) 491-6710. Inexpensive to moderate. Lunch and dinner.

PUNTE DEL ESTE
Argentinean/Uruguayan/Cuban/Mexican/ Oakland Park

You'll really have to resurrect your high school Spanish to spend an evening in this outlet of the Pan American Union—although you can always point to the menu and order the charcoal-grilled steak with fried eggs and yellow rice, the empanada meat pies, homemade sausage, beef tongue with garlic, and Parrillada Criolla, translated on that menu as "Parrillada Criolla." Less challenging to local non-linguists are the tamales and tostones, or the burritos, black beans and rice.

Buenos Aires Plaza, 1678 East Oakland Park Boulevard. (305) 561-3382. Inexpensive. Lunch and dinner.

R.J.'S LANDING RESTAURANT & DOCKSIDE CAFE
American/Fort Lauderdale Beach

An al fresco dockside delight that specializes in seafood starting with stews, salads and jumbo shrimp given the cajun, curried, fried, Rockefeller or scampi treatment. Then come swordfish Oscar, sushi-quality tuna sauteed rare and coated with cracked black pepper; Norwegian salmon with linguine and a creamy pesto sauce; raw bar items and for land-bound palates: steaks, ribs and chicken. Plus—and it's a big PLUS, gator fritters, gator ribs and cracked Alligator Dundee with Hogan sauce.

515 Seabreeze Boulevard. (305) 763-5502. Moderate to expensive. Lunch and dinner.

RAINBOW PALACE ★★★
Chinese/Fort Lauderdale

With more marble than most mausoleums can boast, this professionally served and extremely well cheffed gem is one of the best-looking Chinese restaurants in the country—in the table appointments, the window and floor treatments, the lavish use of fresh flowers. A 1991 mission from New England to an area already choking with chop suey servers, this palace is worthy of its name. We start with Hunan popcorn, lightly battered squid rings, and shrimp with a fine ginger sauce, continuing with lobster, shrimp and scallops in a hot pepper sauce, roast duck stuffed with shrimp pasta and served with an orange Grand Marnier sauce, or anything else on the sophisticated menu.

2787 East Oakland Park Boulevard. (305) 565-5652. Expensive. Lunch and dinner.

THE RAINDANCER
American/Fort Lauderdale

What we like most about this steak house is the upstairs lounge with its cheerfully blazing fireplace—perfect on an almost nippy night as staging area for consideration of the dinners below. But before deciding what to order, check the counter in front of the grill chefs and pick out the cut and size of the meat, remembering that the double-thick pork chops are as good as the steaks. Then hit the salad bar!

3031 East Commercial Boulevard. (305) 772-0337. Expensive. Dinner.

REGAS GRILL
American/Plantation

If you like the Chili's chain approach to running a restaurant of the Mexican-American persuasion, you'll probably like this addition to their portfolio, the only Florida-based link in the mini-chain of a dozen nation-wide. Up to now they've been slow growers, starting in Knoxville in 1919; but with their volume serving of quality food at non-greedy prices they're bound to grow. Pay special attention to heartsmart items, the bisques, mesquite-grilled chicken, creamed spinach, baby back ribs and for finisher, the Applepuff.

Fountains, 809 South University Drive. (305) 452-0010. Inexpensive to moderate. Lunch and dinner.

RENAISSANCE
Seafood/Fort Lauderdale

In the heart of a world class spa and rambling resort with more than 500 rooms, this oasis has been home to a string of restaurants which have been largely unnoticed by the locals because of the location deep in the western boonies. But with the completion of new roads, access is easier, and we have no trouble taking the time when the seafood off the grill is so good—-and kind to the diet.

Bonaventure Resort and Spa, 250 Racquet Club Road. (305) 389-3300. Moderate to expensive. Dinner.

RENE'S ★
Italian/Hallandale

No matter what the status of beef and blood counts, Americans want their steaks, those slabs of meat that come pounding in from the plains. And here's the place to find them, along with knock-out skins-on, garlic-in roast potatoes, crispy and irresistible. The dinner salads are far better than the norm, the garlic dressing sheer heaven, and the garlic bread is blissfully removed from the hero-half, packed pellet school—Rene's secret is the Cuban bread.

3190 West Hallandale Beach Boulevard. (305) 989-9843. Moderate to expensive. Dinner.

RIO VISTA ISLE CAFE ★★
Continental/Sunrise

What a charming little cafe Janet and chef-husband Eric Oswald have put together, a comfy country cabin with lots of class, watched over with great friendliness and honest concern by the calm and quiet Janet. Chef Eric is so talented and honest that we order anything with great confidence, but generally favor a starter course of Danish meatballs, frikadelle, baked stuffed artichokes or a crab cake, more crisply coated than most and served with his own chile and remoulade sauces, much better than most. Then we zero in on the nut-crusted rainbow trout, schnitzel Holstein with its compulsory caper-dotted fried egg, salmon poached or en papillote, a plate of steamed fresh vegetables, duckling with Grand Mariner and Wisconsin sour cherries or the chicken breast served with grilled shrimp scampi, chunks of veal, mushrooms, olives and plum tomatoes—always remembering to save room for his deliciously tempting whipped cream and chocolate desserts.

7836 Northwest 44th Street. (305) 749-8118. Moderate. Dinner.

Best Family Team

The Perrons – Bernard, Kathy, Lisa, Jon, Marc and Jean – Brooks, 500 South Federal Highway, Deerfield Beach.

RISTORANTE NAPOLI
Italian/Pompano Beach

Trattorias don't get any simpler than this one in low-rent restaurant territory, but neither do they reflect more honesty in the preparation and presentation of such Italian-American favorites as chicken cacciatore, veal marsala, linguine with white or red sauce, eggplant parmesan. We order anything with portobellos and look forward eagerly to the night's special desserts, made out back as lovingly as everything else.

1051 East McNab Road. (305) 781-0930. Moderate. Dinner.

RIVERSIDE HOTEL
American/Fort Lauderdale

We put this in the book because we love to have breakfast in the dining room, starting the day with white napery and having our fast-breakers delivered in a quiet, civilized setting, picking up our complimentary Sun-Sentinel as we enter. We also come back for lunch in the cozy fireplace lounge by the International Cafe where the menu concentrates on uncomplicated sandwiches, salads and a few pasta dishes.

620 East Las Olas Boulevard. (305) 467-0671. Moderate. Breakfast, lunch and dinner.

RIVERVIEW
American/Deerfield Beach

This rustic reminder of the good ole days in South Florida, a 1920s packing house converted to a gambling casino, has been beautifully preserved and lovingly tended by Bill Stewart. The walls talk—of guys and dolls and high-rollers—-while you feast on stuffed Florida lobster tail, broiled yellowtail or one of the steaks, set awash with honest drinks and good wines. We come back in daylight hours to watch the boats go by and participate in the fun of the nouvelle California creations.

1741 Riverview Road. (305) 428-3463. Moderate to expensive. Lunch and dinner.

RIVERWALK BREWERY
German/Fort Lauderdale

Fort Lauderdale's own brewery, built by master German craftsmen, manned by master German braumeisters, paid for and owned by German investors-operators who provide a mini Munich Hofbrau Haus setting for snacking, singing, sipping. This multi-million dollar marvel, convenient to the Broward Center for Performing Arts, is a perfect spot for raising a few steins before or after the show—or at any other time. Prosit!

111 Southwest 2nd Avenue. (305) 463-BEER. Inexpensive to moderate. Lunch and dinner.

RIVERWALK EATERY
American/Fort Lauderdale

A fresh breeze from the Keys—casual, laid back and cool—and close to the Broward Center for the Performing Arts. Perfect for pre- and post-theater munching, lunching and dining. The burgers are good, the salads freshly assembled and the sandwiches thickly stacked. At night we like the seafood and chicken teriyaki, and any time the chili and cornbread—a real winner.

215 Southwest 2nd Street. (305) 760-4373. Inexpensive. Lunch and dinner.

ROADHOUSE GRILL
American/Pembroke Pines

The promising beginning of a chain catering to revived appetites for All-American beef, with all the proper surroundings—Western music blaring from the juke box, homey, ole-timey wall hangings, last round-up design with lots of wood inside and out. The steaks are on display in front of the giant grill, so take a gander before you order and settle into your beer, brought to the table in abucket of ice. Nice touch.

8525 Pembroke Pines Boulevard. (305) 438-0599. Moderate. Lunch and dinner.

ROBATA-YAKI HOUSE
Japanese/Lauderdale Lakes

Another of the multi-purpose introductions to the way the Land of the Rising Sun approaches its food. You sit at the sushi bar to admire the chefs rolling the rice with such precision, on a tatami mat to test your joints and muscles, or at table where you can have one of the kimono dressed staff serve the sukiyaki or do it yourself with shabu-shabu and robata-yaki, a fun event for groups.

4340 North State Road 7. (305) 731-7920. Inexpensive to moderate. Lunch and dinner.

RONIERIS ★★★
Italian/Pembroke Pines

The terrific Ronieri twosome, chef Ronald, "Rinaldo", Rabin and son David handling the front room, have returned to the kind of intimate setting they started with in Wilton Manors before getting bitten by the bigger is better bug, working elaborate spots in Miami and Pompano Beach. In this more modest spot we usually start with the raspberry coated chicken wings with foccacio on the side, followed by whatever homemade pasta is featured, and then the chicken or veal saltimbocca, or a fish of the night—grilled, blackened, sauteed, whatever Dave recommends. If we're really being firm about the non-firm figure, we go immediately to the Weight Watchers section of the menu. That makes us feel better about ordering the tiramisu and finishing the last of the wine—the list is lengthy and knowledgeably selected with many vintages available by the glass. Where did the Rabins get the name Ronieri's? They combined Ron with the astrological sign of his wife—she's an Aries.

207 North University Drive. (305) 966-2233. Moderate. Dinner.

Best Espresso Bar

Caffe Roma, 1915 East Atlantic Boulevard, Pompano Beach, where there are Italian papers and Italian TV.

ROSA'S
Italian/Deerfield Beach

Typical of the many family-run pizzerias-plus, this one is owned and operated by the Servidoes, headed by papa Pasquale and Queen Rosa (that's what the mural and her T-shirt say) from Calabrese and their children, Rosetta and Vito. Subs, calzones and strombolis are on the menu along with lots of spaghetti and fairly good chicken cacciatore.

Cove Shopping Plaza, 1636 Southeast 3rd Court. (305) 427-9002. Inexpensive. Lunch and dinner.

THE ROSE & CROWN
British/Fort Lauderdale

If you want to relive that last trip to London, surviving on pub grub to stretch the weakened dollar, head for the never-never land of warehouses in the unlikeliest of places and check into this merrie little corner of England. Order one of the eight excellent ales, lagers, and stouts on tap and after lifting a few, get serious with some bangers and mash, black pudding, steak and kidney pie, fish n' chips. And the next day check with your travel agent and book another trip to London.

3680 West Commercial Boulevard. (305) 731-6245. Inexpensive. Lunch and dinner.

ROYAL INDIA
Indian/Davie

An unlikely location for top-notch Indian fare, but an easy-to-recommend oasis in the midst of all the roadhouses and trailer parks. Start with the wonderful breads—nan, papadum, paratha—covered with chutneys and proceed to some samosas followed by an order of the orange-colored, marinated chicken from the tandoor oven. The lamb curry is also worth the trip but be sure to order the yogurt raita with cucumber or mint, some Indian beer or rosewater to calm those curries. Finish your feast with a firni finale.

3801 Griffin Road. (305) 964-4030. Moderate. Dinner.

RUNYON'S ★★
American/Coral Springs

The telephone number says it all. This is a great place for BEEF. Especially the Tarzan-size slab of prime rib. But it's also a very reliable place for broiled fillets of fresh fish, and nobody in Broward or Palm Beach counties is fussier about their baked potatoes. Large and perfectly prepared Idahos. Not since the days in Chicago when Toffenetti's made a big thing about its Idahos have we tasted better. We also like the non-threatening setting, the smiles of the staff and the professional supervision.

9810 West Sample Road. (305) 752-BEEF. Expensive. Lunch and dinner.

RUSTIC INN CRABHOUSE ★
Seafood/Fort Lauderdale

The originators in the area of what to many people can become an addiction—garlic crabs. They're the beautiful swimmers, the blues of the Chesapeake or Florida or wherever, steamed with lots of garlic, or with Old Bay, or cut up into chunks to put in the crab soup—a superior blend. Come casual because the crabs will be dumped on your newspaper-covered table and you'll do the picking and pounding—mallets provided. Great fun. There's also other seafood, pasta, steaks but we come here for the crabs.

4331 Ravenswood Road. (305) 584-1637. Inexpensive to moderate. Lunch and dinner.

RUTH'S CHRIS STEAK HOUSE
American/Fort Lauderdale

The first name is for the Ruth Fertel who in 1965 bought a New Orleans steak house named Chris and then made it grow and grow and grow and... now there must be three dozen of them in the collection. The menu is simple and of course you have to have beef, but start it off with some seared tuna. Everything but the steak knife is a la carte, so the costs do mount rather quickly.

2525 North Federal Highway. (305) 565-2338. Expensive. Dinner.

SAGAMI
Japanese/Fort Lauderdale

The first Sagami on the causeway was so successful that the owners opened a second a little farther north on Federal Highway and then a third way up north, all the way to West Palm Beach. We frequent all of them, chopsticking our way through an array of the artfully wrapped sushi, dipping into the wasabi-fired soy sauce, wondering who invented tempura, and remembering to say "skeee—aki" when ordering sukiyaki.

5975 North Federal Highway, (305) 771-4447; 1005 Southeast 17th Street, (305) 764-7874. Moderate. Lunch and dinner.

SAGE ★★
French/Fort Lauderdale

An April-in-Paris cafe with a menu that is guaranteed to transport you to the City of Light. Or maybe to Brittany with the various crepes on the menu. Or you can take our route to Rouen starting with French onion soup or the grilled scallop-shrimp sausage in a herb-butter sauce, proceeding to Coquille St. Jacques en Croute, some Coq au Vin or the Cassoulet a L'Armagnac, that Gascon garlic sausage-duck-haricot bean crock of fortification. Finish with one of their special cakes or the chocoholics dream crepe. This is a good value-for-the-money discovery.

2378 North Federal Highway. (305) 565-2299. Inexpensive to moderate. Lunch, dinner and Sunday brunch.

SAIGON ORIENTAL RESTAURANT
Vietnamese/Hollywood

In the simplest of shack-like settings and non-decor, this corner storefront is serving some of the most exciting food to be found in Hollywood—of the ethnic persuasion. Start with one of the soups and work into whatever is the special of the night, seeking the advice of any of the natives who understands English.

2031 Hollywood Boulevard. (305) 923-9256. Inexpensive. Lunch and dinner. Closed mid-July through mid-August.

ST. GREGGORY'S LA FONDUE
Swiss/Fort Lauderdale

Owner Greg Hunsberger started this smelter in 1985, after graduating from the Restaurant School of Florida State. It was a bold stroke, for it was a one-of-a-kind operation which attempted to revive the fondue craze of the 1970s. Fondue and its cousin, raclette, were regular outings for us the five years we lived in Switzerland, but in Florida we find it difficult to fondue in the heat. But the story here, the varieties offered and the wines are good enough to shatter our resistance.

1025 North Federal Highway, Fort Lauderdale. (305) 525-4734. Moderate. Dinner.

Best Happy Hour

The sardined social shopping on Fridays at Bimini Boat Yard, 1555 Southeast 17th Street, Fort Lauderdale, and every night at The Cove, 1755 Southeast Third Court, Deerfield Beach.

SAN ANGEL ★★★★
Mexican/Fort Lauderdale

This best of all Mexican restaurants in South Florida is the happy little storefront empire of the Pria boys with chef Eduardo in charge of the tiny kitchen. There's not a sombrero in sight. Nor a burrito or taco on the menu or any of those combination plates which quickly convert to masses of mush. Instead are such touches of imaginative genius as grilled yellowtail served with avocado and green chili salsa; tenderloin tips with onions in a sharp, smoky chipotle sauce; grilled eggplant filled with goat cheese, onions and jalapenos and baked with an ancho chile sauce; grilled salmon accompanied by poblano peppers, corn relish and lime-splashed garlic butter, sauteed salmon with a walnut-pomegranate cream salute and finally, boneless chicken in a mole sauce made from 27 different peppers. Need I say more?

2822 East Commercial Boulevard. (305) 772-4731. Moderate to expensive. Lunch and dinner.

SANTA LUCIA ★★
Italian/Fort Lauderdale

Few restaurants in this book are such one-person operations as this one. The restaurant is Angelo Ciampi, a transplanted Italian with great energy, conviction and push. Ask him if the fish is fresh, and he'll dangle a pompano or snapper in front of your face. Question the veal chop and his entire inventory will be brought raw to the table. The menu is as abbreviated as the setting, but there is always some grilled fish available, superb soft shells in season, and hopefully, sauteed portobellos. Angelo will guide you—with great gusto.

602 East Las Olas Boulevard. (305) 525-9530. Expensive. Dinner.

SEA SHANTY
Seafood/Fort Lauderdale/Lauderhill

What started as a real shanty in the boonies of Griffin Road was successful enough to warrant a spinoff shanty in Lauderhill. Each of them keeps it simple as management does its best to keep their lines taut and the supply swimming in from the docks. Our standard dinner commences with a crabmeat cocktail, a couple helpings of the salad bowl and then a simply broiled fillet of whatever they promise is fresh.

3841 Griffin Road, Fort Lauderdale, (305) 962-1921;7101 West Oakland Park Boulevard, Lauderhill, (305) 741-8055. Moderate. Dinner.

SEA WATCH ★★★
Seafood/Fort Lauderdale

A brilliant capturing in structure, substance and spirit of just the kind of place visitors hope to find in Florida. An aged wooden trading post smack on the ocean, handsomely but not cutely landscaped, filled with nautical memorabilia, including a terrific gallery showcasing the great age of sail. We start our meals here with some frozen margaritas on the second deck, and then, depending on the weather, move to the outside porch, or stay inside to order our seafood prepared with California flair and brought to table by a bouncing, bubbly crew.

6002 North Ocean Boulevard. (305) 781-2200. Moderate to expensive. Lunch and dinner.

SEAFOOD WORLD
Seafood/Lighthouse Point

Simplest of settings with Bahamian mementos and a fish market alongside. Check out the counter and order your seafood fresh, letting the crew
out back prepare it Caribbean island style with some spices—after you
spoon your way through some of the best seafood chowder this side of St.
Barts.

*4602 North Federal Highway (Main Street Plaza). (305) 942-0740.
Moderate to expensive. Lunch and dinner.*

SEPTEMBER'S
Continental/Fort Lauderdale

Chef Shashank Agtey cooked for First Lady Barbara Bush and Vice-
President Quayle when they roared through town in '92—before the elec-
tion—and if you want their menu order the chicken rollatine, made with a
rolled, boneless breast filled with fresh mozzarella, spinach and prosciutto splashed with marinara. The stuffed veal breast the Veep ate is not on
the regular menu—instead order the giant veal chop served with spaghetti
squash, puffy white rice with a very good creamy sauce generously
bristling with morels. Be sure to start with the Mushrooms Farci—jumbo
crowns filled with cognac-flamed crabmeat—or the carpaccio. Bombay-
born Agtey will also use his expertise to prepare curry dishes in this inner
sanctum isolated from all the wild doings in the large, and loud, lounge
the other side of the brick.

2975 North Federal Highway. (305) 563-4331. Expensive. Dinner.

SHEFFIELD'S
Continental/Fort Lauderdale

Marriott's flagship in South Florida boasts several restaurants of note, but
this sequestered and well-served signature room is the best. Pseudo
English manor house in design, it has numerous romantic escape tables
for two, and an ambitious menu. We like to start with the wonderful lobster bisque or the cheese-spinach ravioli and then move to Dover sole or
the roast rack of lamb, looking forward to something really sinful for
finale.

*Marriott Harbor Beach, 3030 Holiday Drive. (305) 525-4000.
Expensive. Dinner.*

SHELLS
Seafood/Sunrise

Bare bones approach to the serving of seafood, priced at levels guaranteed to bring the crowds and raise the noise level. This is not a place to linger or to do much of anything else except eat—in a kind of gobble-gobble- gulp-and-go-manner. We like the freshly-shucked oysters, the steamed shrimp and the mud pie for dessert.

2019 North University Drive, Sunrise. (305) 749-0557. Inexpensive. Dinner.

SHIRTTAIL CHARLIE'S
Seafood/Fort Lauderdale

Sensational setting on the New River with decks and docks for open-air dining, and terrific views of the old and new— the first hotel from the early 1900s, and the Broward Center of Performing Arts. Enjoy it all while digging into the many excellent noontime salads and sandwiches— we like the blackened cajun chicken mouth-stretcher—or the dinner shrimp-scallop combo given the Caribbean or scampi treatments, the sauteed conch steak or the fisherman's platter, while learning all about Shirttail Charlie.

400 Southwest 3rd Avenue. (305) 463-3474. Moderate. Lunch and dinner.

SHOGUN JAPANESE RESTAURANT
Japanese/Dania

There's a definite homemade look to this little charmer, both outside and in, but that's what we like about it along with the sushi bar. New management took over in mid-92 and they made some menu changes but of course they still serve skillfully assembled rolls, slices of tuna, octopus and snapper sashimi as prelude to tempura and teriyaki treats.

1302 South Federal Highway. (305) 920-7976. Moderate to expensive. Dinner.

SIAM CURRY HOUSE
Thai/Wilton Manors

Back in the 1970s when few South Floridians knew the difference between nam sod and pla prid prig, this was one of the first little feederies to introduce the treats of Thailand to the area. A small army of competing countrymen has now established beachheads but the Curry House is still hanging in there, smiling their way through explanations to those still not aware of the pleasures found in peanut sauces, masaman and panang curries, coconut milk and lemon grass.

2010 Wilton Drive. (305) 564-3411. Inexpensive to moderate. Lunch and dinner.

SILVER PALACE CHINESE RESTAURANT
Chinese/Deerfield Beach

The location next door to the movies guarantees that this palace will not be overlooked as a possible destination before or after the flicks. Its reasonable prices add to the popularity, as does their cross-culinary handling of Hunan and Szechuan specialties as well as Cantonese and Mandarin. We order the crab kissed with ginger and scallions, squid in curry sauce, cold sesame noodles, a whole fish heightened with the spices of Hunan.

3996 West Hillsboro Boulevard. (305) 698-9611. Inexpensive to moderate. Lunch and dinner.

SOUTHPORT RAW BAR
Seafood/Fort Lauderdale

The sustaining slogan here—on door, walls, bumper stickers—is "Eat Fish Live Longer. Eat Oysters Love Longer. Eat Clams Last Longer." Is that why this classic raw bar is always packed with a casual crowd slurping their bivalves and beverages?

1536 Cordova Road. (305) 525-2526. Inexpensive. Lunch and dinner.

SPICED APPLE
American/Fort Lauderdale

A country cabin designed with great imagination and style, a place to have Carolina mountain barbecue and beans plus all kinds of chicken, lobster and steak, catfish, corn fritters, collard greens and of course, spiced red apple sauce. Fun for the whole family, especially those who miss the country and those who have never seen it.

281 Griffin Road. (305) 962-0772. Moderate to expensive. Lunch, dinner and Sunday brunch.

STARBRITE
American/Pembroke Pines

The heyday of the diner is definitely not past, whether retro-fitted for the 50s or jazzed up for the 90s. There is still a need out there for Starbrite meat loaf and mashed potatoes, fruit salads served with date-nut bread, breakfast omelets, pancakes and waffles served all day long—AND good old fashioned soda fountain sins like banana splits.

10041 Pines Boulevard. (305) 431-9551. Inexpensive. Lunch and dinner.

Best Men's Room

Read the wall-poster newspaper accouts of golfing greats at McDivot's, 3011 Rock Island Road, Margate.

STUDIO ONE CAFE ★★★
Continental/Fort Lauderdale

German-born chef-owner Bernd, veteran of the luxury yacht galleys, dropped anchor here with wife-hostess-manager Roberta in 1993. They scrubbed the place clean, added some fine art, spruced up the space and devised a great value-for-the-money menu that's filled with temptations. It's changed regularly, but count your blessings if Bernd is serving gravlaks—the presentation is the best this side of Stockholm. He also does perfectly poached fresh Norwegian salmon in a super dill sauce, osso buco that should send Italian chefs back to the drawing boards, crispy black duckling in vanilla sauce, veal-filled tortelline with vodka-spiked Alfredo sauce, and camembert-stuffed chicken breast with French cranberry sauce. For finishers there's superb bread pudding and the kind of fresh fruit tarts we can seldom find in South Florida.

2447 East Sunrise Boulevard. (305) 565-2052. Moderate. Lunch and dinner.

SU SHIN ★
Japanese/Lauderhill

So successful was the first Su Shin on the 79th Street Causeway in Miami that they cloned two more, in Kendall and North Miami Beach, and then opened this one for the good people of Lauderhill, all those who have learned to appreciate the diet-conscious fare centered around rice and raw fish, along with the beautiful bubbling broth of properly prepared sukiyaki, and the lightest of coverings on the tempura.

4593 North University Drive. (305) 741-2569. Moderate. Dinner.

SUKHOTHAI ★★★
Thai/Fort Lauderdale

You can thank Siriluk, "Susie", Komolsane and Sompong Csanawocsai for this happy trip into the Land of Smiles. As hostess and chef they were the team that made Wilton Manors' Siam Cuisine something to write Bangkok about and now they're doing the same wonderful work here, with Susie smiling around the front room and Sompong brewing platonically perfect chicken coconut soup, making scallops with sweet basil, and the kind of curries we always want to encounter.

1930 East Sunrise Boulevard. (305) 764-0148. Moderate. Lunch and dinner.

SULTAN'S KEBABS
Middle Eastern/Hollywood

Located in the Young Circle swing of ethnic exotica, this Mid-East marvel has no sultan or Sadam, but it does have a full range of the kind of food found in many countries east and south of the Mediterranean—hummus, tabouleh, stuffed grape leaves, and of course the namesake kebabs—our favorite is the lamb. There's also an array of the sweets that Beirut used to be famous for, and a huge TV screen for watching VCRs of belly dancers on the nights there are no live navel maneuvers.

1824 Harrison Street. (305) 927-0002. Inexpensive to moderate. Lunch and dinner.

SUSHI BLUES CAFE
Japanese/Hollywood

You want funky? Slow-shufflin' saxophone with your sashimi? Soft drum tempo with teriyaki and tempura? This is very definitely the place, a simple little storefront with galactic mural outside and sushi bar inside, a few tables and a kitchen that does wondrous variations on standard Japanese themes. Good enough to make you want to jump up and sing anything but the blues. Kenny Millions is the musician and his wife the wiz out back making her own orchestrations of dumplings, smoked sausages, soft shell crabs with sesame sauce—it's a wonderment. They even had chamber music and Mozart a few moons ago.

1836 South Young Circle. (305) 929 9560. Moderate to expensive. Dinner.

SWISS CHALET
American/Oakland Park/Pembroke Pines/Lauderhill

Nothing fancy here, just lots of food at bargain basement prices served by a staff that never stops bustling back and forth with the consistently good chicken and rib dishes, produced in volume and consumed in volume.

601 East Commercial Boulevard, Fort Lauderdale, (305) 776-1630; 301 North University Drive, Pembroke Pines, (305) 966-2604; 1870 North State Road 7, Lauderhill, (305) 735-8831. Inexpensive. Lunch and dinner.

TAKEYAMA ★
Japanese/Plantation/Deerfield Beach

When the Miami Dolphins made their 1991 trip to Tokyo for an exhibition game, Kenny Takeyama was there to cheer on his team, and to guide South Florida media through the Tokyo Fish market, largest in the world. Just as he's been guiding Gold Coasters through the intricacies of his Japanese kitchens, stir-frying the crunchy vegetables, crispifying the tempura seafood, marinating his meats teriyaki style.

6920 Cypress Road, Plantation, (305) 792-0350; 300 South Federal Highway, Deerfield, (305) 427-9491. Moderate. Lunch and dinner.

Best Dinner Show

The Mai-Kai of course, longest running Polynesian review in the nation, 3599 North Federal HIghway, Fort Lauderdale.

THAI GARDEN ★
Thai/Margate

Main man here is Dan Sangpukdee who has put together a very pleasing garden of great delights, one in which we have great confidence in anything we order, but usually succumb to yet another serving of the do-it-yourself satay with one of the best counterpoint set of side dishes devised in any country's cuisine—slightly sweetened cucumber slices and a spicy peanut sauce. After that beginning we march onward to something with red, green or panang curry, or the fried whole snapper with ginger and peppers.

Carolina Springs Plaza, 7950 West Sample Road. (305) 755-2199. Moderate. Lunch and dinner.

THAI PEPPER ★★
Thai/Coral Springs

Opened in March 1991 by Mike Ponluang, a familiar name to all those Thai-atics who learned to rely on his Commercial Boulevard Thai Express. Before that he was in London's Chelsea running a snack shop. Now he's in charge of a class operation, handsomely furnished with window treatments, carefully fitted paneling and moulding that would win prizes in Bangkok. And good housekeeping awards anywhere—this place is painstakingly—and proudly—maintained. And it's well supplied with excellent food—non-greasy soups, superlative nam sod and egg rolls, garlic shrimp, sizzling duck, and much, much more.

2049 University Drive. (305) 341-6912. Inexpensive to moderate. Lunch and dinner.

THAI SPICE ★★★★
Thai/Oakland Park

Main man here is Eddie Tatton and you'll recognize his face if not the name if you've been to the Mai Kai any time since the mid-1960s—he was the maitre d' there for 30 years. Here, in this 52-seater next door to a Thai grocery with an express take-out service, he's joined by his son Michael, head chef, who's assisted by his talented wife and a team that knows how to prepare Thai classics with the kind of finesse and delicacy not often encountered when Thai-ing one on. We can recommend anything on the menu or verbalized as a special of the evening, but we especially like the soups, curry puffs, the pompano steamed in a ginger-scallion sauce and served over a medley of fresh vegetables, and the whole yellowtail snapper coated with a crisp cover of chili garlic sauce freckled with freshly chopped cilantro and scallions.

1514 East Commercial Boulevard. (305) 771-4535. Moderate. Lunch and dinner.

Best Maitre d'

James Deering is the master of his craft at Chameleon, 1095 Southeast 17th Street, Fort Lauderdale.

THREE GUYS FROM ITALY
Italian/Plantation

A double header, with one and a half of the three guys in a simple store-front pizzeria and one and half next door running a restaurant with more than a few stabs at elegance. We get our midday submarines in one place and from the shared kitchen order the homemade cheese ravioli and man-icotti, the shrimp fra diavolo, scungili marinara, veal picante or the let-it-all-hang-out zuppa di pesce.

New River Plaza, 1663 South University Drive. (407) 475-1480. Moderate. Lunch and dinner.

TIJUANA GRANDE
Mexican/Lauderdale Lakes

Superlative Mexican and Spanish cuisine in a simple yet artfully decorat-ed and carefully maintained room with the abiding presence of Dianna Maholland who's in charge along with her brother, Mario Berbotto. They were raised in Uruguay where their Italian grandmother passed family recipes to Dianna, who uses them now to make the excellent salad dress-ing and the flan made with cream cheese and lemon sauce. We've never tried the "Wild and Crazy Tostado," but we can vouch enthusiastically for the garlic-creole shrimp.

4345 North State Road 7. (305) 731-5297. Inexpensive to moderate. Lunch and dinner.

TINA'S SPAGHETTI HOUSE
Italian/Fort Lauderdale

Opened in 1951, this institution has had several owners, all doing the same thing—serving at non-greedy prices, generous portions of spaghetti, lasagna, pizza, calamari and a good house-made creamy garlic salad dressing.

2110 South Federal Highway. (305) 522-9943. Inexpensive. Lunch and dinner.

TOONZ
American/Sunrise

A cool gathering place for the 20s—30s set who want a South Miami Beach kind of setting, but with a new twist—toonz, as in cartoonz. They're shown non-stop in television sets everywhere, like a sports bar. What the heck! It's better than waiting until Saturday morning and while you're watching you can munch on Buffalo wings or loaded tater skins; chicken in sandwiches, salads, and smothered with mushrooms, onions, provolone; or you can bite into one of their burgers named Bam Bam, Scooby Dooby, Superman, Tweety and Yosemite Sam. Thaaaaats all Folks!

3543 North Pine Island Road. (305) 742-8863. Inexpensive to moderate. Lunch and dinner.

TROPICAL ACRES
American/Fort Lauderdale

Here's one of the veterans, a thriving survivor since 1949 and still serving reliable charbroiled steaks aged and cut on the premises, but also good seafood, pork and lamb chops and some Italian specialties.

2500 Griffin Road. (305) 989-2500. Moderate. Dinner.

TRULLO'S
Italian/Pompano Beach

Chef-owner Charlie Perrone is heir to a family restauranting tradition that goes east to Doria's Pier V and Villa Perrone in Hallandale, and the menu he's developed for this ristorante across from the Palm-Aire complex has many similarities with those successes. Skip the starters and get down to the main action, the 30 entrees, giving the veal al Trullo a try—medallions sauteed with artichokes and mushrooms, olives and onions. The chicken scarpariello is my favorite and chef Charlie knows how to prepare it—the sauce does not flood the dish but is absorbed into the chunks of chicken and sausage.

Parkway Plaza, 1280 South Powerline Road. (305) 977-9375. Moderate. Dinner.

TRY MY THAI! ★★
Thai/Hollywood

If the name doesn't suit you, consider Kiss Me Squid, Try My Legs, Young and Tender, and A Fish Called Wanda. They're all on the menu of this little bit of Bangkok in a mod setting. Their explanation of the star system for degrees of spiciness is a classic. Among our favorites here are the Baby Drumsticks with a red sauce at once sweet and peppery, the Pad Thai rice noodles mingled with chicken, shrimp, garlic, coriander, lime; and the Forever Shrimp saluted with ginger and shrimp paste.

2003 Harrison Street. (305) 926-5585. Moderate. Lunch and dinner.

Best Al Fresco Barstools on the Highway

The row in the great outdoors a few feet from the traffic at the Riptide, 1309 South Federal Highway, Fort Lauderdale.

TUMI RESTAURANT
Peruvian/Hollywood/Oakland Park

Peruvian food? Sure. Not exactly what the natives were living on when the conquistadors arrived but a fusion of cross-cultural cuisine. Start your introduction with some of the papa a la huancaina, a curiously flavorful combination of potatoes, chili and cheese, and then get ready to spoon into a stew, one made with chicken, lamb or rabbit. The setting on Johnson street is casual to the core but there's live entertainment nightly, as there is at the much more elaborate spread in Oakland Park.

5917 Johnson Street, (305) 985-8358; 1666 East Oakland Park Boulevard, (305) 561-1472. Moderate. Lunch and dinner.

TUTTI'S AT WESTON
Italian/Sunrise

Why not do dinner and a movie? This cafe with Italian trattoria aspirations is close to the flicks and has some innovative touches—smoked mozzarella-stuffed ravioli in a tomato cream sauce, a good selection of pastabilities along with New York strip steaks and fresh slabs of tuna. The spiffy service is another extra.

Indian Trace Center, 1342 Southwest 160th Avenue. (305)389-5200. Moderate. Lunch and dinner.

Best Ice Cream – Broward

They all scream for ice scream at Jaxson's, 128 South Federal Highway, Dania.

TWO GUYS ★★
Italian/Fort Lauderdale

What owner John Marks started in 1977 as a 47-seat pizzeria is now a 200 seat full-scale restaurant after its latest million dollar expansion in 1993—bar, patio, dance floor, computerized take-out service which just might be the most efficient pizza operation in the country. We go for the luncheon grilled chicken-mushroom-lettuce-spinach-raspberry dressing salad and the hoagie with marsala-sauteed sirloin strips topped with mushrooms, mozzarella and onions then baked beautifully brown. Later in the day we start with seared rare tuna with peppercorns and crispy onions in a saffron sauce, followed by wood plank-roasted grouper served with polenta and grilled tomato relish; or the grilled veal loin and lobster pairing served with a white zinfandal vanilla bean cream sauce. The wine list is OK with 14 of the 32 labels served by the glass. Like we said, this is more than a little ole pizza parlor.

701 South Federal Highway. (305) 462-7140. Inexpensive to moderate. Lunch and dinner.

UMBERTO'S
Italian/Pembroke Pines/Fort Lauderdale

Umberto I decided to open Umberto II on Oakland Park but later sold it, so there are now two owners. But they both believe in the same solid kind of Italian fare the Americans have learned to love. Starting with pizza and ending with cannoli and spumone. Good savings for the early bird diner.

1320 North University Drive, Pembroke Pines, (305) 432-5056; 2100 East Oakland Park Boulevard, Fort Lauderdale, (305) 566-5226. Inexpensive. Dinner.

VESUVIO
Italian/Pompano Beach

One of the smallest eateries in the book, impossible to miss with its over-size outside wall painting and the words "Neopolitan Cuisine". This is unabashed Southern Italian, straight from New York's Little Italy—that's where the chef-owners learned their lessons well. We admire their pride in performance, and origin. When's the last time you saw an Italian restaurant advertise it wasn't Northern?

420 North Federal Highway. (305) 941-1594. Moderate. Dinner.

VICTORIA PARK
Cajun/Fort Lauderdale

Named for the area in which it takes up such a small amount of space, this tiny spot decorated in vibrantly happy colors of the Caribbean has had many chef-owners over the years, each of whom were obviously fer-vent believers in reincarnation. The current occupants take cross-culinary paths, mixing a little—or maybe a lot—of Cajun peppers and spices for coating their seafood, but also mingling their pasta with vegetables, shrimp, scallops, and sauteeing some of the best calves liver we've had anywhere in the area.

900 Northeast 20th Avenue. (305) 764-6868. Expensive. Dinner.

VILLA BRUSCO
Italian/Pompano Beach

There seems to be no end to the number of Italian restaurants, cafes, pizza parlors and places with greater or lesser degrees of posh in South Florida; but there's always room for someone who's doing pasta, garlic-sauteed shrimp, broiled fillets of fish, osso buco and other veal classics without compromise or inflated prices. The cooking here is Calabrese and it's very good.

4190 North Federal Highway. (305) 941-1012. Moderate. Dinner.

Best Sports Celebaurant

Dolphin running back Mark Higgs calls the plays at Higgy's Goal Line Cafe, Sunset Mall, Sunrise..

VILLA GRAZIE
Italian/Pembroke Pines

You'll be singing the name of this place as you leave, after indulging in plate after plate of the American-Italian classics, the linguine with red or white clam sauce, ravioli, angel hair and other featured farinaceous fare, chicken cacciatore, and good veal dishes, accompanied by a forest of garlic sticks, followed by more homemade goodies—cannoli, cheesecake and the still trendy tiramasu.

11252 Pines Boulevard. (305) 431-0492. Moderate. Dinner.

VILLA PERRONE
Italian/Hallandale

A palace of marble, statuary, fountains that recalls the good old days of Miami Beach baroque, but serving as a tribute to and by the Perrone family which has fed thousands in the area. The service is tuxedo-formal and friendly while remaining thorough-going professional—and Italian. The food is top quality, with no surprises—snapper Francese, veal Milanese, chicken marsala, broiled scallops with lots of butter, strip steak pizzaiola.

906 East Hallandale Beach Boulevard. (305) 454-8878. Moderate to expensive. Dinner.

VILLA ROSE
Italian/Hollywood

It's nothing more than a storefront in the midst of storefronts that have nothing to do with food, but behind the simple entry is some of the best pizza—the thin crust species—to be found anywhere on the Gold Coast. And that's the reason it's in this guide.

1114 North State Road 7. (305) 981-5622. Inexpensive. Lunch and dinner.

VINCENT'S ON THE WATER
Italian/Davie

Sam Boubsikos and his wonderful wife, Aphrodite, returned to take back this free-standing blockhouse in the late 80s, bringing new life to the scene of their former triumphs and installing a menu with seafood as the specialty. I like the combination creations with their harvests from the deep and I like the salad boat with freshness and pride of presentation as appealing as the seafood.

3445 Griffin Road, (305) 961-5030. Moderate. Dinner.

Best Vietnamese Restaurant – Broward

The family act at Nam Long, 4461 North State Road 7, Lauderdale Lakes

WAN'S MANDARIN HOUSE ★
Chinese/Fort Lauderdale/Hollywood

Davie Wan is the master of this house and he's honoring a family restauranting tradition in South Florida that goes back to 1966 when his father opened the first Wan's Mandarin House on Southwest 8th Street in Miami. Davie's peregrinations have taken him to so many other locations we wondered if he shouldn't buy a mobile home. But in these two locations he seems to be settled, and now that he has his own son working in the house, the tradition is going to continue and that means top quality Chinese food.

1201 North Federal Highway, Fort Lauderdale, (305) 561-1888; 3331 Sheridan Street, Hollywood, (305) 963-6777. Inexpensive to moderate. Lunch and dinner.

WATERFRONT
American/Hillsboro Beach

Behind the statue of the famous Barefoot Mailman, past where the wonderful ship replica Mary Celeste bar used to be—before the big fire—this cafe with its rehabilitated piano bar features a good salad bar, a solid menu of seafood specialties plus the usual land-locked entrees, and oceanfront views through the wall of windows.

Barefoot Mailman Hotel, 1061 A1A. (305) 785-8110. Moderate. Lunch and dinner.

THE WHALE'S RIB RAW BAR
Seafood/Deerfield Beach

A whale of a place with nautical nonsense all about, a small bar-counter, tables and booths wedged into odd corners, and a kitchen on view shucking-frying the clams and oysters, rolling the conch fritters, layering the sandwiches which they serve on whole wheat buns. The Buffalo style whale wings are great, as are the snails, steamed shrimp and salads.

2031 Northeast 2nd Street. (305) 421-8880. Inexpensive. Lunch and dinner.

WILD ROSE CAFE
Continental/Hollywood

Opened in the spring of 1991 by a dedicated couple, Sheila and John Jacob, who don't mind being tucked into the corner of an office complex way off the beaten eaten path, this cafe is their second time around. They struggled for a time in Long Island's East Hampton. It's a great success story: John starting as a dishwasher at Key West's Pier House, getting to Hyde Park's Culinary Institute, serving as chef to Kentucky Governor John Brown. His menu is on a changed-daily blackboard and the running-back-and-forth Sheila will do the explaining. You'll be lucky if he's doing garlic-cheese bread, perfect with egg drop soup, chicken breast Greek or scampi style, and Louisiana Pie, a quiche kind of conglomerate with shrimp and a spicy, peppery custard fill. Pasta, roast beef au jus and mesquite-grilled New York strip can also be on the menu.

North Park Executive Suites, 2699 Stirling Road. (305) 962-7447. Moderate to expensive. Lunch and dinner.

WINDOWS ON THE GREEN
American/Fort Lauderdale

There's a regular rotation of menus in this signature restaurant, and that's nothing but good news to the locals who want to keep coming back to this civilized spread of windows looking over the carefully trimmed landscape. When we last had that privilege we marveled at the lime and tequila zapped seafood ceviche, the wild mushrooms with herbs and the essence of veal, and the corn-crab chowder with grilled andouille.

Pier 66, 2301 Southeast 17th Street. (305) 525-6666. Expensive. Dinner.

Best Diner – Broward

The Katsenos clan's Olympia Flame, 80 South Federal Highway, Deerfield Beach.

THE WINE CELLAR ★
Hungarian/Fort Lauderdale

The same wonderful couple, Lui and Viki Behofsits who pleased so many value-for-the-money seekers over the years in Dania's Old European Restaurant and then the Alpine Village on Lauderdale's Commercial Boulevard, charged back into the fray in June, 1993. This setting is the best of the three with fountains, a glassed-in aviary plus bunches of grapes and barrels, and Hungarian-born chef Lui making the rounds. Start with a cold fruit soup as prelude to the gulyas—goulash—the crisp-roasted duckling or chicken paprikash. Save room for the strudel.

199 East Oakland Park Boulevard. (305) 565-9021. Inexpensive to moderate. Dinner.

YESTERDAY'S ★
Continental/Fort Lauderdale

A high energy very today kind of place, with a wall of windows overlooking the Intracoastal, cozy corners for privatizing, and an extensive menu noon or night—with the Sunday brunch a real eye-full. The rest of the week we like to start our dinners with roast gator bits, followed by terrific Caesar salad, veal Bacchus, sauteed with madeira- soaked mushrooms and finished with heavy cream, or the cioppino, made famous by the Italian fishermen working the wharf in San Francisco.

3001 East Oakland Park Boulevard. (305) 561-4400. Moderate to expensive. Dinner.

ZUCKERELLO'S
Italian/Fort Lauderdale

A gymnasium-size mass feeder with a lot of spiffy service and a menu that just won't quit—20 individual-size pizzas, 26 pastabilities, and then such tempters as shrimp scampi or gratinati, mussels posilippo—one of our favorite orders— veal scallopine Florentine, chicken or eggplant parmesan, lamb chops in garlic butter sprinkled with parsley. Basta!

3017 East Commercial Boulevard. (305) 776-4282. Inexpensive to moderate. Lunch and dinner.

Palm Beach Area Restaurants

This section lists in alphabetical order 219 restaurants in Palm Beach County. Restaurants in the following cities are included:

Boca Raton
Boynton Beach
Delray Beach
Greenacres
Highland Beach
Hypoluxo
Lake Park
Lake Worth
Lantana

Manalapan
North Palm Beach
Palm Beach
Palm Beach Gardens
Palm Springs
Riviera Beach
Singer Island
West Palm Beach

A & B GRILL
American/Boynton Beach

Spotless little cafe with spiffy service and a good variety of salads, sandwiches and burgers. In a mall which has more than its fair share of vacancies, this cafe thrives.

1701 North Congress Avenue. (407) 364-7105. Inexpensive to moderate. Lunch and dinner.

ABACO'S
Seafood/Lantana

An ultra casual raw bar with all the extras—pool table and wide-screen TV, daily drink and food specials, weekend live entertainment. The bivalves are freshly shucked and the shrimp are fried, scampified or delivered for peel 'em yourself action. There's also pasta, burgers and grilled chicken breasts.

Atlantis Plaza, 6186 South Congress Avenue. (407) 641-0373. Inexpensive. Lunch and dinner.

ABBEY ROAD
American/Lake Worth

Years ago there were several well traveled Abbey Roads and this is the last one to survive in its present format—super salad bar, consistent kitchen producing solid steaks and seafood, with early bird savings, friendly service and congenial atmosphere. Another plus is the live entertainment in the lounge.

7306 Lake Worth Road. (407) 967-4852. Moderate to expensive. Lunch and dinner.

ABBEY ROAD GRILL AND SPORTS EMPORIUM
American/Palm Beach Gardens/Delray Beach

Popular sports bar complete with all the necessaries— battery of TVs, dart boards, and a bouncy, bustling, superfriendly staff setting the right tone for the ultra-casual atmosphere. Munchies and finger food are the main event here but there are also sandwiches, burgers and the kind of steak specials delivered in vintage Abbey Road style, plus an excellent array of Caesar salads.

10800 North Military Trail, Palm Beach Gardens, (407) 775-7556; 710 Linton Boulevard, Delray Beach, (407) 278-6622. Inexpensive. Lunch and dinner.

Best Diner – Palm Beach

Ellie's 50s Diner, neon neat and super friendly, 2410 North Federal Highway, Delray Beach.

ADDISON'S FLAVORS OF ITALY ★★
Italian/Boca Raton

The flavors are certainly there, from the stunning cart of starters, featuring roast peppers, seafood salad, eggplant and a crepe-layered torte, to the entrees of snapper Livornese, veal piccata, rigatoni mingled with salmon and tomatoes splashed with vodka and finished with cream, filet mignon with goose liver pate and Madeira sauce. But the setting is strictly Addison Mizner. The painstakingly restored buildings, which served as architect Mizner's administrative headquarters during the 1920s, are on the National Register of Historic Places. Chef-owner Joe Cordaro should have a place of honor in the Boca Register of Preservationists for keeping this model of adaptive restoration so vibrantly alive.

2 East Camino Real. (407) 391-9800. Expensive. Lunch, dinner and Sunday brunch.

ALEXANDER'S
American/West Palm Beach

From dawn to dusk you can hunker into this roadhouseand order farm-size breakfasts, served up with grits and beaten-out-back biscuits, beautiful, beautiful biscuits.Come back at noon for home-brewed soups, mouth-stretching sandwiches on bread better than most, and at dinner for the kind of food that's now the rage—-meat loaf, stuffed cabbage, mashed potatoes, roast meats.

2690 South Military Trail. (407) 439-6204. Inexpensive. Breakfast, lunch and dinner.

ALEYDA'S
Mexican/West Palm Beach/North Palm Beach

What a success story! Aleyda started with a taco truck in South County, made enough pesetas to open her own cantina in North Palm Beach, and then a second in West Palm Beach, both characterized by very friendly service and Tex-Mex marvels, everything from burritos to tamales, chili rellenos to tostadas, and her sensational empanadas, those marvelous little half-moons filled with spicy meat and potatoes.

1890 South Military Trail, West Palm Beach, (407) 642-2500; 545 Northlake Boulevard, North Palm Beach, (407) 844-0770. Inexpensive to moderate. Lunch and dinner.

AMBER'S
American/Boca Raton

A landmark building which was one of Boca's first restaurants—many owners ago—and which is now a popular spot for those who like to dine and dance. There's a keyboard vocalist nightly. Menu highlights include chicken and veal parmesan, lobster, salmon, dolphin, snapper. This is not a place for the high rollers of today's Boca or the glitterati, but for those more modest types who remember the good old days.

5910 North Federal Highway. (407) 994-2230. Moderate to expensive. Dinner.

ANCHOR INN
Seafood/Lantana

Pleasant setting on a small lake just west of I-95 and featuring seafood from more distant waters. Start with one of their chowders and then order a whole fish served family-style smack in the center of the table on a giant platter. The salad dressings are good, the desserts a delight, especially when key lime and mandarin orange pies are available. For a breath of the bayou, drop anchor with baked fish Creole style.

2810 Hypoluxo Road. (407) 965-4794. Moderate. Dinner.

THE ANNEX
American/Delray Beach

Owners Bob and Linda Allen do all they can to live up to their boast that they have "Olde Fashioned Food at Olde Fashioned Prices", defining those words with meat loaf and roast pork, prime rib, Key West salad with grilled chicken breast, broiled dolphin and all kinds of luncheon salads and sandwiches. They leave the ice tea pitchers on the tables. The setting is informal in a nice kind of way with a clientele not seen along the ocean. A great value- for- the-money discovery.

301 Northeast 3rd Avenue. (407) 243-2816. Inexpensive to moderate. Lunch and dinner.

APPLAUSE
French/Delray Beach

Chef-owner Rene Lague moved to this quiet corner of Delray in 1992 after responding to an ad in a local paper in his hometown of Meilhan in the Garonne, Aquitaine. He took the plunge, making his first trip to U.S., going directly to this kitchen where he's doing his French thing—sea bass prepared in sea salt and served with white butter, French onion soup, shrimp salads with raspberry vinaigrette, chicken breasts in cherry-mushroom sauce, duckling with sauce Royale and a fillet of beef with red wine. We like best his poached Atlantic salmon with sauce veloute, chopped shallot sprinkled butter with chives, chevril and tarragon.

640 East Atlantic Avenue. (407) 274-9003. Moderate to expensive. Dinner. Closed June through September.

THE ARK
American/Lantana

Come by the twos, threes, fours or alone to this popular non-boat which doesn't get too silly exploiting the name. They have a fine lunch buffet Monday through Saturday, and for dinner, straightforward fried and grilled seafood, roasts and chops preceded by as many roundtrips to the salad bar as your appetite and capacity allow.

2600 Lantana Road. (407) 968-8552 and (407) 968-8552. Moderate. Lunch, dinner and Sunday brunch.

ARTURO'S RISTORANTE
Italian/Boca Raton

A tutto Italiano experience with the Gismondi family in charge. Papa Arturo is the patriarch, son Vicenzo, "Vinnie", the maitre d' and son Giuseppe, "Joe", the chef with his son Arturo at his side. Check the pasta and seafood selections available that evening as you enter and head for our favorite porch room which in spirit takes us back to Harry's Bar in Venice. The formal staff moves with precision, delivering the best of all appetizer arrays—-don't pass up the Torta Primavera with its 13 layers of antipasto. Among the highlights are the roasted peppers, the bread, snapper livornese, veal chop, osso bucco and whatever is recommended by the captain, Vinnie or Joe. Excellent Italian wines.

6750 North Federal Highway. (407) 997-7373. Expensive. Lunch and dinner.

AUBERGE LE GRILLON
French/Boca Raton

Eve Churches, who had been in the restaurant for years, inherited this Inn of the Cricket from Harm Meyer and Malcolm Miller, and in 1993 made major improvements in both front and back dining areas. Whether you start with lobster bisque or salmon coubliac and then move on to veal chop with garlic-leek sauce, duckling with apricot and Grand Marnier, or grilled tuna in ginger-shallot butter, a special highlight is the wonderful vegetable plate set in the center of the table family style. The desserts are heavenly.

6900 North Federal Highway. (407) 997-6888. Expensive. Dinner.

BACI
Italian/Boca Raton

High Tech black and white cafe with lots of granite, Lucite and neon, a dramatically arranged wall of wine, on-view theater kitchen and beautiful counter food displays. Caesar salad with oak-grilled chicken, ravioli in a veal ragout, and the salmon in a fine champagne sauce served with fresh spinach and leeks are among our favorite selections. Our favorite seating is outside where the noise level is not so distracting and the people watching is great.

Plaza Real, Mizner Park. (407) 362-8500. Moderate. Lunch and dinner.

BANANA BOAT
American/Boynton Beach

A waterway-hugging oasis where the view of the boat parade is sensational, the waitresses better than those at Hooters and the food passable. Favorites here are the conch fritters and conch chowder, cobb salads, jambalaya rice and fresh catch of the day simply broiled. Lunch is my favorite trysting time although the weekend brunches and the evening reggae are fun.

739 East Ocean Avenue. (407) 732-9400. Moderate. Lunch and dinner.

BANGKOK HOUSE
Thai/West Palm Beach

When you feel the need for a pla prad fix or a bit of palate-tingling ground pork-white onion nam sod make this neatly appointed house your home. We order anything with the coconut milk-cooled curries or the grilled whole fish in hot sauce. The settings are a bit dressier than most of the competition and the staff is all smiles.

Concourse Plaza, 2062 Palm Beach Lakes Boulevard. (407) 471-7711. Moderate. Lunch and dinner.

THE BASIL GARDEN   ★
Italian/Boca Raton

Double storefront ristorante with a touch of class and friendly feelings. Here we start with New Zealand mussels marinara, have a bit of angel hair with garlic and oil before settling into a breaded veal cutlet in the Milanese manner or scallops of veal wrapped around fontina and spinach. The black suited waiters are an experienced bunch, concerned with your well-being and satisfaction.

5837 North Federal Highway. (407) 994-2554. Expensive. Dinner.

BASIL'S NEIGHBORHOOD CAFE   ★★★
American/West Palm Beach

Omnipresent owners Donna and Uwe Roggenthein keep this place exciting. The chefs are partially on view working under a giant blackboard of the day's specials. From beginning to end it's a triumph, from the first drops of herbed olive oil on the bread to such finishers as macadamia chocolate tart. In between, we have reveled in such pleasures as garlic-blackened sea trout with tomato-infused gnocchi, roasted garlic, and tomato salsa all on a bed of steamed spinach; and the roasted peppers, shrimp and mascarpone on grilled rye bread, with a pasta salad and assorted bits of fruit.

771 Village Boulevard. (407) 687-3801. Moderate. Lunch and dinner.

BEN'S STEAK HOUSE
American/West Palm Beach

Here's the classic roadhouse-steakhouse from yesteryear, a non-fussy, non-theme, no-decor kind of darkened hideaway, with spacious booths ringing the walls and some greenery here and there, especially around the 50-plus item salad bar. The portions from the plains range from chopped sirloin to thick slabs of quality prime rib. Chicken, liver, and some seafood are also on the menu but at Ben's you think beef, beef, beef.

3400 South Congress Avenue. (407) 967-3400. Moderate to expensive. Lunch and dinner.

BENNARDO
Italian/Delray Beach

Andrew and Josephine Bennardo fled the rigors of the north in 1992 and turned into restorers, transforming a 1925 home into a cozy little restaurant, one watched over with great pride and TLC by hostess-manager Josephine. Out back, chef Andy does his Italian thing with great gusto, filling angolotti with asiago and chopped duck, slicing paper-thin carpaccio and grilling portobellos, infusing shrimp with ginger, and producing Straw and Hay Pasta Elena, named for his mother-in-law and consisting of green and white noodles sporting chunks of lobster.

116 Northeast Sixth Avenue. (407) 274-0051. Expensive. Dinner. Closed June through August.

BENVENUTO
Continental/Boynton Beach

Alain Betton and Phillips Cherrualt are the extra caring French duet in charge of this attractive reminder of an earlier Florida, the Mediterranean headquarters of the kind of tropical garden attraction that was popular in the 1940s. The lush landscaping forms an inviting canopy entrance and dramatically lighted backdrops on view from the main dining rooms. The menu is not all gator and possum however, but Bahamian conch chowder, house pate, fried calamari, veal T-bone with popover, filet mignon, French-cut lamb chops, Swiss-style potatoes. Wrap it all up with warm apple pie a la mode.

1730 North Federal Highway. (407) 364-0600. Moderate to expensive. Dinner and Sunday brunch.

BICE RISTORANTE
Italian/Palm Beach

The first Bice opened in Milan in 1926 and the ninth Bice in Palm Beach 64 years later, serving a varied menu of pleasers: carpaccio, salmon ravioli, veal Milanese, stewed stuffed quail with polenta and porcini, grilled tuna in the Sicilian style. It works hard to become the "See and Be Seen" fun spot in town from its enviable location in the heart of one of the great shopping and strolling streets of the world.

313 Worth Avenue. (407) 835-1600. Expensive. Lunch and dinner.

BISTRO L'EUROPE
Continental/Boca Raton

The same dynamite duo of Norbert and Lidia Goldner, he a German and she a Brazilian, opened this handsomely appointed gem—the most civilized setting in Mizner Park—as a sophisticated spinoff from their Cafe L'Europe in Palm Beach. Linger at the upfront bar while reviewing menus and surveying the dazzling dessert table and then cozy into a booth and order snapper encrusted with gauze-like potato straws, osso bucco, wienerschnitzel or any of the specials. Good wine list with many labels available by the glass.

Plaza Real, Mizner Park. (407) 368-4488. Expensive. Lunch and dinner.

BOHEMIAN GARDEN
Continental/Lake Worth

High volume feeder with Eastern European accents on the seafood, fowl and meats, with prime rib, wienerschnitzel, duckling and roast loin of pork among the featured attractions. There's a Milwaukee roadhouse feel to the place, a homey friendliness about the veteran staff, and maybe the kind of beer garden feeling a few of you might remember from yesteryear.

5450 Lake Worth Road. (407) 968-4111. Moderate. Dinner.

BOSTON'S
Seafood/Delray Beach

Capital of casual cuisine across the street from theocean and a magnet for the younger set flocking for the live music once the sun goes down. Noon and night it's a magnet for seafood lovers who crave the kind of clam chowder and lobster clam bakes New England made famous. The salads and sandwiches are also good and the open-air porch is great for people-watching any time, starting with breakfasts on the weekends.

40 South Ocean Boulevard. (407) 278-3364. Moderate. Lunch and dinner.

BRAMAN'S RAW BAR AND GRILL
American/Delray Beach

Jeff and Pete are the amiable owner-operators who oversee an all-day former HoJo with good burgers, club sandwiches and munching food like popcorn shrimp, clam strips and conch fritters in addition to the usual raw bar items. Get serious at dinner with T-bones, New York Strips and baby back ribs.

115 Northeast 6th Avenue. (407) 278-7573. Inexpensive to moderate. Breakfast, lunch and dinner.

Best Desserts – Palm Beach

The incomparable carrot cake and other treats at Cafe Floresta, 183 West Camino Real, Boca Raton.

BRANDYBURGER
American/Boynton Beach

33 (Count 'em T*H*I*R*T*Y*T*H*R*E*E!) burgers to choose from and they are served with superior regular or seasoned (garlic and paprika) French fries, good slaw and tomato-white onion garnish. Beautiful to look at, wonderful to consume and consistently top quality—thanks to Nat Brandel who's been perfecting his performance since opening in March 1987.

Boynton Trail Center, 9804-E 8, South Military Trail.(407) 736-8008. Inexpensive. Lunch and dinner.

BRITTANIA ARMS
British/Boca Raton

Boca's only English pub, opened in 1993 and featuring authentically prepared fish n' chips, steak and kidney pies, British beers on tap and by the bottle, with cream teas in the afternoon and on Sundays roasts, lamb and beef with Yorkshire pudding. An intimate piece of Bonnie Britain.

2399 North Federal Highway. (407) 655-6611. Moderate. Lunch and dinner.

BUSCH'S
Seafood/Delray Beach

Yes, it's the same name and, for the most part, the same people who used to be on A1A in Ocean Ridge. And they're still specializing in seafood, grilling and broiling their fillets, dressing up the shrimp and brewing chowders. But now they've go a much better location, right on the Intracoastal, and an outdoor patio where you can sit and enjoy that view.

892 Atlantic Avenue. (407) 278-7600. Moderate to expensive. Dinner.

CAFE AL FRESCO
Italian/Boca Raton

Al fresco in name and spirit only, created by a wall-filling mural that transports the diner to the beautiful Bay of Naples while other walls are filled with windows overlooking the landscape of beautiful Boca. The decor is trattoria-happy, the service super friendly and the menu Sicilian and Southern Italian, although the American origins of the family in command, the Borrellis, are in East Meadow, Long Island.

21073 Powerline Road. (407) 483-5400. Moderate to expensive. Dinner.

CAFE CHARDONNAY
American/Palm Beach

One of my favorite restaurants in France is Le Chardonnay in champagne country and one of my favorites on these shores proudly bears the same name, but their kitchen handles Italian and Southwest American favorites as well as French. Start with one of their designer pizzas, some chili or a strudel filled with seafood, and then move on to that San Francisco bouillabaisse known as cioppino, lobster tangled with linguine, calves liver, leg of lamb. For a fabulous finisher, order chocolate cake with raspberry sauce. What to drink? Chardonnay of course.

Garden Square Shoppes, 4533 PGA Boulevard. (407) 627-2662. Moderate to expensive. Lunch and dinner.

CAFE D'JAN
American/Lantana

Outdoor-indoor deli with a good variety of non-deli items—-seafood platters, catch of the day—-along with children's menu, display counter filled with High Cal desserts, and breakfast that's served from 7 a.m. until 4 p.m. They make a pretty good stab at a Philly cheese steaksandwich and their gyro with a dozen slices of meat and a garden salad is layered on to, not into, the pita.

225 East Ocean Avenue. (407) 588-7495. Inexpensive. Breakfast, lunch and dinner. Closed July through mid-August.

Best Hotel Dining Room – Palm Beach

The Ocean Grand where super chef Hubert Des Marais makes magic, 2800 South Ocean Boulevard, Palm Beach.

CAFE DU PARC   ★
French/Lake Park

Since 1980 this free-standing house three miles south of PGA Boulevard has been the happy home of Pierre and Anne-Marie Latuberne, she in the front and he out back. Together they create a provincial charmer that is not too French, too cafe, too cute, but a solid achiever offering such standbys as beef Wellington and duckling au poivre, shrimp scampi, rack of lamb and veal Normande. Small, select wine list.

612 Federal Highway. (407) 845-0529. Moderate to expensive. Dinner.

CAFE FLORESTA ★★★★
American/Boca Raton

The Campbell clan is responsible for this stunner which opened in 1993 after months of on-site planning, restoration and construction; and after years of preparation. The Campbell's catering service, A Matter of Taste, has been top of the line for years, giving them all the experience needed, and the perfected recipes, to open a class restaurant. This is certainly that, but it's also a casual neighborhood kind of place, inspired in its design by Boca's Old Floresta section where the Campbells have lived in one of the Addison Mizner houses for more than 30 years. The sense of place is definitely here, as is the sense of being welcome and well taken care of by one of the best staffs in all of South Florida. They deliver with great pride—and knowledge—the comfort foods reflecting a regional American approach—a litter of fritters (corn, cheese and conch), steak and potato salad, black bean soup with confetti rice and essence of Persian lime, grilled vegetables, slow-fired smoked chicken with plantation style buttermilk spoon bread, sage-stuffed pork chop with wild mushrooms, peppered rib steak with sauteed watercress. The desserts are incredible, the best in the county and arguably the best in South Florida—nowhere have we had better carrot cake.

Camino Square, 183 West Camino Real. (407) 368-5370. Moderate to expensive. Lunch and dinner.

CAFE GLORIA
French/Boca Raton

Vest-pocket feedery boasting a more extensive menu than one expects to find, with lots of pasta and seafood and highly personable service. Gloria is the sweetness and light out front and Jean-Louis is the chef whose head and shoulders you can see through the counter space as he bustles about in the very definition of postage stamp kitchen.

Boca Bank Building, 855 South Federal Highway. (407) 338-9692. Moderate. Lunch and dinner.

CAFE L'EUROPE ★★★★
Continental/Palm Beach

The quintessential restaurant for Palm Beach, one with all the built-in elegance and elan, watched over ever so professionally by Lidia and Norbert Goldner overseeing a staff with great class and menu with dash. Start withthe caviar assortment in the upfront bar, perfect for sipping a bit of the bubbly and popping fish eggs while deciding if you want to start your meal with the flawless lobster bisque, garlic-laden escargot, smoked trout with creamed horseradish garnished with apples and onions, or the phyllo-wrapped baked brie with an apple coulis and slices of kiwi. To be followed by potato-encrusted snapper with shaved baby fennel in a garlic-spiked beurre blanc, pennette pasta with roasted eggplant and seasonal vegetables blessed with basil, or a Black Angus strip sirloin with red wine reduced sauce and an onion confit with chevre-filled baked potato. The desserts are sheer heaven, especially the fruit tarts. The wine selection is as praiseworthy as everything else in this Worth Avenue treasure.

150 Worth Avenue in The Esplanade, Worth Avenue.(407) 655-4020. Expensive. Lunch and dinner.

CAFE MONTEREY ★
American/West Palm Beach

Phil, Cottie, Suzanne and chef Rich are the crew that's in charge of this cozy little cafe convenient to library, Intracoastal and all the action downtown on and off Clematis. In a mod cafe setting they're serving what they call "Progressive American Cuisine," defined as grilled beef tenderloin with wild mushrooms; Maine lobster with grilled shrimp, fresh vegetables and pasta; grilled breast of chicken with artichoke hearts, mushrooms, roast peppers and mushrooms in a herb-infused brown sauce, or stuffed with a unique melange of almonds, fennel, mushrooms and sausage in natural sauce. The side dish of butternut squash with a blob of pesto in the center is a real winner.

123 Clematis Street. (407) 659-1914. Moderate to expensive. Dinner.

CAFE OLE' ★★
Mexican/Boca Raton

For starters we like the oysters dusted with cornmeal and black pepper and served with a papaya salsa or the nachos "Supremo"; for salads the Caesar and for the main action, Montezuma pie layered with chicken, mushrooms, cheese and tortillas with a red chile sauce; and the grilled, jazzed up top sirloin covered with gaucho rings and accompanied by black beans. Ole' for the cafe!

Arvida Parkway Center, 7860 Glades Road. (407) 852-8063. Moderate. Dinner.

CAFE ON THE PARK
Continental-Finnish/Lake Worth

Here's a blast from the past, Finnish-American style—a pinker than pink dining room in a restored pink palace with superb location on park and lake. Go back to the 1920s in spirit while the Finnish owners provide their own interpretations of continental cuisine starting with lightly smoked salmon with dill potatoes and ending with cloudberry parfait or marzipan-coated cake. In between are poached salmon in a cognac-spiked light cream sauce and other fillets of fresh fish.

Gulfstream Hotel, One Lake Avenue. (407) 586-9250. Moderate to expensive. Breakfast, lunch and dinner.

CAFE PROTEGE
New American/West Palm Beach

This display kitchen and 150-seat dining room of the Florida Culinary Institute opened in February, 1993 as a showcase for culinary arts students. And what a showcase! Designed by the same restaurant designer Adolfo Galvez responsible for such stunners as Mark's Place and the Shula successes in Miami, and Maxaluna in Boca Raton. Cuisines featured will range the world, but concentrate on regional American with such New Wave twists as grilling fresh salmon on applewood then serving it with passion fruit sauce and tropical fruit salsa; pairing veal steaks with goat cheese in a red wine sauce mingled with caramelized onions.

2400 Metro Center Boulevard. (407) 842-8324. Moderate to expensive. Lunch and dinner.

CAFE ROMA
Italian/Delray Beach

Immaculately maintained and very friendly thimble-size cafe with a surprisingly ambitious menu featuring penne pasta in a vodka-spiked pink tomato sauce, shrimp, mussels, clams and squid marinara or fra diavolo over linguine, chicken with eggplant and cheese, veal piccata or parmesan.

20 East Fifth Avenue. (407) 276-0966. Inexpensive to moderate. Lunch and dinner.

CAFFE D' ITALIA
Italian/Boca Raton

A spinoff from the owners' popular pizzeria next door with a menu which features homemade farinaceous fare, veal marsala and parmesan, sole francese and marinara, chicken rollatine or scarpariello and pretty good cheesecake and tiramisu.

Palmetto Park Square, 1367 West Palmetto Park Road. (407) 392-3338. Moderate. Dinner.

CANTON GARDEN
Chinese/Boca Raton

Not nearly as elaborately furnished as several of the other Chinese feederies in the area—in fact it's close to a non-decor—but that does not prevent us from dropping in for a simple lunch built around budget happy specials. At dinner time we gladly return for one of the best preparations of the General Tso chicken classic, a Happy Family combination featuring shrimp and scallops, or lobster Cantonese.

Spanish River Plaza, 500 East Spanish River Boulevard. (407) 395-2029. Moderate. Lunch and dinner.

Best Cole Slaw – Palm Beach

The freshly-assembled melange at Ellie's 50s Diner, 2410 North Federal Highway, Delray Beach.

CASABLANCA CAFE
Continental/Palm Beach

Main man here is Nikiforos Stoupas who opened this bit of cafe fun in a 1936 Art Deco gem that used to house a soda fountain. Now it's a fountain of diet-conscious fare along with a few specialties to do honor to Nick's native Greece, and such standbys as luncheon pizza and burgers. The dinner menu changes nightly, so consider yourself lucky if your night in Casablanca (Please don't "Play it again Sam," to the waiter), Nick's kitchen, with chef Alan Krausse in charge, is doing the roast lamb redolent of rosemary or a fillet of fresh fish crusted with onion and tickled with thyme.

101 North County Road. (407) 655-1155. Moderate. Lunch and dinner.

CHARLEY'S CRAB
Seafood/Palm Beach

Chuck Muer made this his first crab outpost on the Gold Coast and then went on to establish other Charley's Crabs north in Jupiter and south in Fort Lauderdale. Decor is nautical without being nonsensical, the staff is well- trained and eager to please. Selection of fresh fish changes with the luck of the catch, but there's always a good parade of pastas, stir-fried vegetables, buttered skins-on red potatoes with flecks of parsley, a few items for land-locked palates, and an interesting array of starters.

456 South Ocean Boulevard. (407) 659-1500. Expensive. Lunch, dinner and Sunday brunch.

Best Maitre d' – Palm Beach

Peter Scheuerl is in top form at The Grill at the Ritz-Carlton, 100 South Ocean Boulevard, Manalapan.

CHEF RETO'S
Continental/Boca Raton

Geo Classical Cuisine is what owner chef Redo Demarmels and his long-time partner Jon Reed call their style of cooking, "marrying the ideology and techniques of classical cooking with available local ingredients and exotic foods from around the world," as they put it and then prove their point with fillets of fresh grouper concealed in a light potato crust accompanied by orange rouille, grilled zucchini, roasted baby artichokes and a basil-eggplant tapanade; sweetbreads flattered by a rich brown gravy and served with fresh spinach; sauteed fresh pompano lightly sprinkled with capers and croutons with diced lemon;roast lamb bedded down with sirtakis and couscous. There's a risotto of the night and some other pasta offerings, perfectly arranged salads of endive and greens, and desserts that are the ideal conclusion to such a display of talent—a remarkable chocolate pudding with banana and strawberry slices and orange zest, tiramisu given a bracing shot of cointreau, and the largest portion of creme brulee, a veritable soup bowl, in Florida.

41 East Palmetto Park Road. (407) 395-0633. Expensive. Dinner.

CHUCK AND HAROLD'S
American/Palm Beach

Founders Chuck Muer and Harold Kaplan are both gone, but this remains part of the Muer corporation, meaning it has the kind of menu found in the Charley's Crab operations. Seated in the sidewalk section, best for serious people-watching, we start with green chile-spiked smoked chicken quesadilla or baked goat cheese with raspberry-tomato salsa, followed by artichoke-shrimp tangled with linguine, Maryland lumpmeat crabcakes, a thick cut of swordfish or yellowfin tuna or the roast saddle of monkfish—not found on many menus anywhere—served with a fine Pommerey mustard sauce and a clump of wilted spinach. Small wine list with eight vintages available by the glass.

207 Royal Poinciana Way. (407) 659-1440. Moderate to expensive. Lunch, dinner and Sunday brunch.

CITRUS ★
New American/Boca Raton

A South Florida cafe with California Dreamin'—mod and minimalist with a good wine list, cool serving staff and a chef who takes his inspiration from California, offering his latest discoveries on three and five-course degustation menus. The pasta combinations are noteworthy, the soups superior and the desserts outrageous. In the right season, the outdoor tables are the only way to go.

4400 North Federal Highway. (407) 394-0007. Moderate to expensive. Lunch and dinner.

CLAUDIO'S BORSALINO
Italian/Lake Worth

I'm not sure if owner-chef Claudio Trevisan wears a borsalino instead of a toque when he's steaming his mussels and mixing his marinara, layering the lasagna and mingling the vegetables and seafood with the pasta, but why not? We tip ours in salute to anyone able to provide the American-Italian classics at such budget-pleasing prices.

Shoppes of Lake Worth, 6669 Lake Worth Road. (407) 433-2376. Inexpensive to moderate. Dinner.

THE COLONY HOTEL
Continental/Palm Beach

As special an experience as The Breakers, though minuscule in comparison, it's the favorite watering hole of a good many Palm Beachers during the season. With two dining areas, the Cotillion Room for tableside flash and fixed price menus of Continental persuasion, and the Grille Room for more casual, bistro-style setting and an American a la carte menu, it appeals to all kinds of diners, including those who like to move to the groove. There are two dance floors and a band nightly.

155 Hammon Avenue. (407) 655-5430. Expensive. Dinner and Sunday brunch.

COPPOLA'S
Italian/Boca Raton

The founders of this modern trattoria, next door to Uncle Tai and across from Tio (Uncle) Pancho in the restaurant-packed courtyard of Crocker Center, have fled to Crocker Mizner Park where they're responsible for the successful Baci. A Korean owner now pays the bills here, keeping the same menu and some of the same staff, smiling their way around the tables outside and in, working in the display kitchen along the back wall. The menu is an extensive one, with most of the old standbys represented along with a superb collection of wines, including most of the Italian headliners.

Crocker Center, 5250 Town Center Circle. (407) 368-7400. Expensive. Lunch and dinner.

THE CRAB POT
Seafood/Riviera Beach

Strategically situated on a bank of the Intracoastal, this seafood shack with chickee hut attached and a sensational porch deck underwent a major rehab in 1991. Start with the smoked fish dip or Chesapeake crab soup with a splash of sherry, broiled sea scallops, a fresh catch fillet or shrimp cooked in beer sprinkled with Old Bay seasoning. For dessert go the whole nine yards and order the sizzling apple pie dolloped with Haagen Dazs and spiked with brandy sauce.

386 East Blue Heron Boulevard. (407) 844-CRAB. Moderate. Lunch and dinner.

Best Italian Restaurant – Palm Beach

Arturo's where four generations of Gismondis are in command, 6750 North Federal Highway, Boca Raton.

THE CRAB POT'S OLD HOUSE ★★
Seafood/Lantana

A kissin' cousin of the Crab Pot and serving excellent crab cakes, conch fritters, beer-blessed shrimp, seafood tangled with pasta, a bottomless salad bowl, and absurdly rich desserts. The baker is on view past the entrance with its museum settings inside the oldest house in Lantana, vintage 1889. That kind of association is enough for most restaurants, but this old house also enjoys what is arguably the best waterfront setting in the entire state. Down the private dock a few conch shells is the ultra-casual raw bar with picnic tables and the always popular chickee bar.Running the whole show is the ever-present Captain Bob.

300 East Ocean Avenue. (407) 533-5220. Moderate. Lunch and dinner.

CROC'S
American/Boca Raton

A classy, popular bar and grill Florida style with large screen TVs, happy hours and early bird freebies, live entertainment and dancing, plus a fine menu featuring coconut-coated fried shrimp, chargrilled fillets of fresh fish, good burgers and ribs. Management here displays a lot of moxie in making their moves with staff and supervision.

Palm Plaza, 22191 Powerline Road. (407) 750-8569. Moderate. Dinner.

THE CUBAN CAFE ★
Cuban/Boca Raton

Established in 1991 by former IBM-er Carlos Rico, who's furnished his happy little cafe with a good deal of style, making the tables and counter himself and selecting all the art work. We do our work here spooning into black bean soup with its covering of chopped onions, then move to shredded beef or the kind of marinated and slow-roasted pork competent Cuban kitchens do so very well. We also like the plantain chips, the championship Cuban sandwiches and the several touches of Puerto Rican culinary traditions.

Plumtree Centre, 3350 Northwest Boca Raton Boulevard. (407) 750-8860. Inexpensive. Lunch and dinner.

CULINARIA GOURMET CAFE
American/Boca Raton

Owners Jill Evans and T. R. Robertson, the chef, have created a cafe with great style. The menu is a weekly affair but consider yourself fortunate if you're there for dinner when T.R. is doing the cheese-garlic shrimp with blue corn polenta, designer pizzas, pasta co-habitating with seafood and for finishers, the Grand Mariner chocolate cake.The menu is extensive for such a small cafe—60 items including 14 heart smart selections. Our favorite is the Moroccan chicken salad, a striking assemblage of cucumber and tomato, celery and various lettuces all serving as base for the grilled chicken dressed with a fine lemon-garlic blend and sprinkled with lots of bulgar wheat.

Colony Shoppes, 7400 North Federal Highway. (407) 994-4300. Moderate to expensive. Lunch and dinner.

CYPRESS MANOR   ★★★
Continental/Boynton Beach

A surprise of the first rank, with a kitchen watched over with great skill by executive chef Randolph Reiss. His bisques are beautiful, the made-out-back sausage served with roasted peppers sensational and the baked shrimp unique, a welcome escape from the omnipresent shrimp scampi routine—stuffed with a fine pesto and fresh mozzarella secured with a wrap of prosciutto. The roasted free range chicken bathed in fresh herbs is in the same big leagues as are the one-pound New York strip steak, grouper aioli, lamb and pork chops, mixed grill, accompanied by oven roasted baby red bliss potatoes and perfectly cooked vegetables. The desserts provide the final reason for putting the Manor on the Gastronomic Grand Tour. The service is more friendly than formal and there's a non-stop Bobby Astor kind of talent at the piano bar—Reginald Asberry.

512 North Federal Highway. (407) 364-0292. Expensive. Dinner.

DAMIANO'S AT THE TARRIMORE HOUSE ★★★
Continental/Delray Beach

In 1993 those dedicated refugees from New York's Russian Tea Room, Anthony and Lisa Damiano, moved their unique act into this carefully restored 1924 memory bank, one-time home of two-time mayor Jack Saunders. It's across the street from Delray's four-acre renaissance of Old School Square but it doesn't offer old-timey Florida fare. Trans-continental and Florasian is what they call their cross-cultural culinary amalgamation of flavors and fancies, such zingers as pan-seared yellowtail crusted with ginger and served with stir-fried Oriental vegetables, and teriyaki-soaked chicken breast coated with sesame seeds and accompanied by potato pancake. To honor their days at the Russian Tea Room, there's chicken Kiev and beef Stroganof. Lisa's desserts are dy-no-mite!

Pineapple Grove District, 52 North Swinton Avenue. (407) 272-4706. Expensive. Dinner.

DAMIANO'S CHILI FACTORY
Southwest American/Delray Beach

A unique little storefront, serving a quintet of organic chilis in what owners Lisa and Tony Damiano of Damiano's at the Tarrimore House claim is "the funkiest, neatest, bestest, chili joint in South Florida". You'll have to get the fire extinguisher if you order the Santa Fe Hot, Hot, Hot Chili, as the menu warns. The black-bean jalapeno stuffed quesadillas are OK but we like more the Catch of the Day Flats, a kind of fajita with chunks of fish sauteed with onions and sweet peppers and covered with jalapeno-flecked cheddar and Monterey Jack. The beer list is fun, the desserts just as wonderful as those Lisa creates at the Tarrimore.

432 East Atlantic Avenue. (407) 274-4177. Inexpensive. Lunch and dinner.

Best French Restaurant – Palm Beach

St. Honore', *tout* French and *tout* terrific, 2401 PGA Boulevard, Palm Beach Gardens.

DAVID CASE'S STREB'S
American/Boynton Beach

The setting is reminiscent of a first class American Plan hotel in the Borscht Belt, very neat and tidy, pleasantly served by a young staff bringing fillets of carefully broiled snapper, salmon and dolphin, lamb chops and steaks. Live entertainment and dancing Friday and Saturday. A popular place for group functions.

2320 South Federal Highway. (407) 734-3033. Moderate to expensive. Dinner.

Best Sushi – Palm Beach

Sagami, 871 Village Boulevard, West Palm Beach, is sure a sight for shore eyes.

DEGREZIA ★
Italian/Manalapan

Another spinoff from New York, opened in 1992 in the heart of a strip of shops that's all posh. The ground floor piano bar provides a welcome introduction and the outside tables overlooking the Waterway a marvelous Florida setting. Upstairs there's an equal amount of downtown elegance and a staff of matching waiters bringing the house specialties— breast of capon Dijonnaise, double-cut veal chop with fresh sage and a pan-fried chop with arugula, endive and radicchio absorbing the natural meat juices; Dover sole meuniere, prime sirloin sauteed in Barolo with a mass of mushrooms. The wine list is a good one and during performances at the neighboring Lois Pope Theater, this is a perfect staging area, especially for lunch before a matinee. Their noontime menu is a complete one, with bountiful fresh salads and fillets of fresh fish that are treated with respect and knowledge.

250 South Ocean Boulevard. (407) 547-0100. Moderate to expensive. Lunch and dinner.

DEMPSEY'S
American/Palm Beach

Amiable owner George Dempsey has been a fixture on the local pub scene since 1977 when he became bartender, then manager, at Doherty's. Eleven years later he opened this spot in the historic Slat House, featuring a large screen TV and the old favorites from Doherty's—chicken pot pie, corned beef hash, steak and eggs, broiled fish, baked crabmeat-stuffed shrimp and chocolate walnut pie.

Royal Poinciana Plaza, 50 Coconut Row. (407) 835-0040. Moderate to expensive. Lunch, dinner and Sunday brunch.

DON PEPE II
Cuban/Mexican/Delray Beach

A spinoff of Don Pepe I in Fort Lauderdale and launch pad for Don Pepe III in Pembroke Pines, with the same kind of reliable Cuban-Mexican fare, everything from black beans and white rice to chimichanga, roast pork and chicken creole to tacos and enchiladas, yellow rice and shredded beef to burros and tostadas. The specialty of this Don is arroz con pollo, chicken and rice served with platanos maduros, sweet bananas. Call ahead to order it—it's made form scratch and takes 45 minutes, well worth the wait.

4755 West Atlantic Avenue. (407) 499-2221. Inexpensive. Lunch and dinner.

ELLIE'S 50'S DINER
American/Delray Beach

Where else in restaurant land can you look a waitress straight in the eye and say "I Want a Whole Lot of Lovin'"or whisper softly "Take a Chance On Me", "Make Me Your Baby"? The first brings mushroom burger, the second grilled ham and cheese, and the third made out back lasagna. It's all part of fun of this neon-neat winner run by Ellie and Bob, who keep a close watch on everything, proud of the consistency of their kitchen. Nobody in the county has better cole slaw and their version of a grilled chicken Caesar is sensational. We also like the burgers.

2410 North Federal Highway. (407) 276-1570. Inexpensive. Lunch, dinner and weekend breakfast.

ELWOOD'S
American/Delray Beach

A textbook example of adaptive restoration of the do-it-yourself school, this former gas station close to the railroad tracks is a great place for ribs southern style, good barbecue beans and slaw, great Cajun catfish bits and comparable collard greens.

301 East Atlantic Avenue. (407) 272-RIBS. Inexpensive. Lunch and dinner.

ELYSEE'S BEACH GOURMET
French/Delray Beach

Great place for a light salad, croissant-wrapped sandwiches and tempting desserts—on display inside where you should view such sinful choices before making your decision about what to eat on the spot and what to take home.

1118 East Atlantic Avenue. (407) 272-9263. Inexpensive. Breakfast and lunch.

ERNY'S
American/Delray Beach

The ultimate old shoe spot, loved by the locals noon and night. Not even the move to classier, spacier digs across the street from their original home could take away the feelings of sheer comfort and caring concern by the veteran staff of waitresses, bringing such All-American fare as burgers, steaks and broiled seafood. Nightly entertainment and a jazz festival in the summer adds to the appeal.

1010 East Atlantic Avenue. (407) 276-9191. Moderate. Lunch and dinner.

EUROPEAN DELICATESSEN ★
German/Lake Worth

Delightful old-world deli German style with shelves of imported items from the Fatherland and glass counters stocked with all kinds of cheeses and top quality sausages, the kind of sandwich-filling stuff we used to call "cold cuts". While Heidi holds court behind that display, husband John is out back making sausages and the waitresses are delivering remarkably good potato pancakes and potato salad, brewed-out-back pea soup, superior sauerkraut, a luncheon salami sandwich that is too generous to believe. On Friday and Saturday nights they serve dinner, featuring schnitzels, sauerbraten, and the kind of wurst that is surely the best. All at pocketbook-pleasing prices.

402 North Dixie Highway. (407) 588-8052. Inexpensive. Lunch and dinner.

EXPLORERS
Continental/Palm Beach Gardens

Signature room in one of the class acts of the county, handsomely dressed in soothingly sophisticated tones and fabrics, with an interesting yet understated gallery of famous explorers looking down from the walls. Superior service and cheffing with such headliners as lamb carpaccio, loin of venison, salmon with a corn-tomato salsa, smoked quail from Bresse blessed by tarragon-spiced sabayon and the ultimate creme caramel.

PGA National Resort, 400 Avenue of the Champions. (407) 627-2000. Expensive. Dinner.

FENG LIN
Chinese/Delray Beach

The name means beautiful maple forest but for me it spells the classics of the American-Chinese kitchen, be they Cantonese, Hunan or Szechuan, prepared with more care than taken by the lesser members of the chopstick crowd. My favorite dishes here are the Hunan whole fish with lots of ginger, chicken with cashews, lamb and scallions and the always superior hot and sour soup.

Old Harbor Plaza, 1725 South Federal Highway. (407) 278-6225. Inexpensive to moderate. Lunch and dinner.

FIFTH AVENUE GRILLE
American/Delray Beach

An upscale English tavern owned by Boynton Beach's Banana Boat bunch with a smiling staff that delivers good Bahamian conch chowder and Bermudian onion soup along with harvests from land and sea. We like the delmonico steaks, the center cut pork chops with a dab of their own barbecue sauce, the grilled swordfish steak bearnaise and the fillet of red snapper sauteed with leeks and mushrooms in white wine and lemon butter.

821 Southeast Fifth Avenue. (407) 265-0122. Expensive. Lunch and dinner.

FIREHOUSE
American/Boca Raton

Fire engine cab in the bar, firefighters' gear hanging on pegs, a parade of fire hats and emblems here there and everywhere, neatly arrayed in a building cleverly designed as—-you guessed it!—-a firehouse. Everything's here but Smokey Stover. Family groups love the prices and All-American meat, potatoes and seafood selections plus the salad bar.

6751 North Federal Highway. (407) 997-6006. Moderate. Dinner.

FLORENTINE DINING ROOM
American/Palm Beach

Palm Beach's premier and most historic hotel boasts this overwhelming dining room that's still something to savor and save for. There's the big band sound and dancing, just like the old days, and the wine list is a good one. Start with a mushroom strudel or one of their special salads and then order a grilled fresh fish of the day, the rack of lamb dijonnaise, filet mignon or Maine lobster. For an eye-popping Sunday brunch, check into the Beach Club dining room.

The Breakers, One South County Road. (407) 655-6611. Expensive. Dinner and Sunday brunch.

FOTO'S
Italian/Boca Raton

No! Don't bring your rolls of film here for developing, but do drop in for pizza New York style. Or a freshly-assembled sub or something more ambitious, such as eggplant parmesan, chicken cacciatore. You can come here before or after watching the action at the Caldwell Theater, or getting your driver's license. It's around the corner from the theater and the license bureau.

7881 North Federal Highway. (407) 997-8190. Inexpensive. Lunch and dinner.

FOUR SEASONS OF BOCA
Continental/Boca Raton

Egyptian Ahmed Gawad is in charge and he puts to good use his experiences as chef and captain. His menu holds few surprises, with the house specialties of rack of lamb and chateaubriand, but we find comfort in familiarity, starting with mussels marinara or clams oreganato, moving on to a veal paillard or piccata, Dover sole meuniere or chicken sauteed with artichokes, garlic, shallots and mushrooms finished with chardonnay.

Kingsbridge Plaza, 5500 North Federal Highway. (407) 998-0802. Expensive. Lunch and dinner.

FRENCH CAFE AND PATISSERIE OF BOCA
French/Boca Raton

Cozy, crowded place for a continental breakfast, ordering the croissants and Danish from the counter a few feet from the tiny tables. Return for luncheon sandwiches, salads and great souffles. Standing by the display counters with all those beautiful pastries and cookies while waiting for a table is the ultimate test of will power.

Royal Palm Plaza, 507 Mizner Boulevard. (407) 391-2575. Inexpensive. Breakfast and lunch.

FUJI
Japanese/Boca Raton

Attractively designed outpost of impeccably prepared sushi and sashimi, best consumed at the bar where you can watch the ambidextrous chefs go through their paces. Then curl into a tatami mat for the fun of do-it-yourself shabu-shabu, sukiyaki and yakiniku, making certain you can see your chiropractor first thing in the morning.

22191 Powerline Road. (407) 392-8778. Moderate. Lunch and dinner.

THE GALLEY
American/Highland Beach

Why a Holiday Inn restaurant in this guide to the best? Because it has a unique oceanfront location a few feet from the surf and is staffed by some of the friendliest folk in the hospitality world, and because they are serving food that's way above the motel average. At noontime we like the seafood casserole, cheeseburgers with lots of red onion and the spinach salad; and at night the budget-pleasing specials on fish, steaks and chicken. The Sunday brunch is also a treat.

Holiday Inn, 2809 South Ocean Boulevard. (407) 278-6241. Moderate. Breakfast, lunch, dinner and Sunday brunch.

GASPAR'S
American/Delray Beach

Opened in the summer of 1993 in a much-used and sometimes-abused restaurant spread, this rambling newcomer might just be able to break the spell of non-success. The salads are as fresh as they are generous in size and the sandwiches are real mouth benders. We also like the burgers and the steaks and their handling of fresh seafood, not to mention the gator bits and gator ribs—a fine conversation stopper when taking snowbirds here.

1111 East Atlantic Avenue. (407) 274-9320. Moderate. Lunch and dinner.

GAZEBO CAFE
★★★★
Continental/Boca Raton

Superwoman Kathy Sellas makes it all happen in this unique jewel box with its spacious booths, springtime decor and formal staff delivering a marvelous menu that encompasses tastes and textures as varied as oysters migonette, Scottish smoked salmon, crabmeat-filled avocados, poached chicken breast hollandaise, tournedos bearnaise, and fresh seafood—bay scallops provencale, Florida red snapper Florentine and Dover sole almondine. The pride of the North Sea is flown in fresh daily from Amsterdam. In season her ultra capable captains fillet upwards to 90 sole a night. And they deliver spectacular desserts—the puffy pillows of raspberries are our favorite. There's a counter with stools facing the galley of chefs whisking their wonders in the original little room of the restaurant—a perfect place to bring a boring companion or amateur chef. Good wines.

4199 North Federal Highway. (407) 395-6033. Expensive. Lunch and dinner. Closed August.

Best Vegetarian – Chinese

The meatless marvels at the Pine Garden, 1668 North Federal Highway, Boca Raton.

GENTLEMAN JIM'S
American/Boynton Beach

Family steakhouse 1990s style, the last remaining link in a mini-chain that made a small rattle across the Gold Coast a few years back, a reliable place to order steaks and some seafood without having to worry about dressing for the occasion or checking with your banker.

2403 South Federal Highway. (407) 734-2244. Moderate. Dinner.

GIACOMO'S
Italian/Delray Beach

So many Italian-American expatriates have opened restaurants on the Gold Coast that we wonder if there are any Italian restaurants left in New York and New Jersey. The Calicchio brothers, Angelo and Anthony, are two of the latest arrivals, opening this bright and airy trattoria in 1993. They take turns in the kitchen, on view in the back brewing a very good clam chowder that's thick and creamy and spiked with tomato and basil, grilling salmon and other fish fillets with roasted garlic sauce and turning out an excellent Pollo Rollatini, breast of chicken filled with several cheeses mingled with mushrooms and spinach and smothered with mushroom sauce. The baked mashed potato cake and julienne of fresh vegetables accompanying are also above average and the brothers blend a pretty good tiramisu.

Harbor Plaza, 1705 South Federal Highway. (407) 279-9464. Moderate to expensive. Dinner.

GIORGIO'S
Italian/Boca Raton

A blockhouse in the unlikeliest of places behind a Winn-Dixie but filled with the charm and enthusiasm of Giorgio, who has created walls of memories about Boca's active theater life, and who sings Italian-American ballads when the spirit moves him. And you can sing your way through humungous family combo platters with all things American-Italian, or such Giorgio specials as shrimp, veal and steak with a little extra spicing.

200 West Camino Real. (407) 0368-3292. Moderate. Dinner.

GRECIAN ISLES ★★
Greek/Delray Beach

Opened in August, 1993, this immaculate and handsomely outfitted evocation of the best culinary traditions of the Cradle of Civilization quickly established itself as the finest Greek restaurant in Florida this side of Tarpon Springs. We like the complimentary ouzo and appetizers brought as soon as you sit down, the flaming saganaki cheese drama, the whole yellowtail charbroiled with lemon, oregano, and a side dish of cooked endive, the rack of lamb, shrimp Mykonos style meaning with feta, tomato and Greek herbs, the clove-infused baklava and the Greek salad, horiatiki, served properly without lettuce but a harvest of garden fresh cucumber, tomatoes, onions, peppers and a shower of wonderful Greek olives. The staff is both professional and pleasant and the Greek wines the perfect complement.

Linton International Plaza, 660 Linton Boulevard. (407) 276-1739. Moderate to expensive. Lunch and dinner.

Best Potato Pancakes

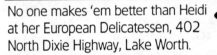

No one makes 'em better than Heidi at her European Delicatessen, 402 North Dixie Highway, Lake Worth.

GREEK VILLAGE
Greek/West Palm Beach

With an Angela Drakontaidis as owner you might expect to find this village well outfitted in Greek blue and white, travel posters extolling the beauties of the Greek islands, and the kind of souvenir stuff one finds all over the strollers' paradise in Athens called the Plaka. But the name also spells such outpourings from the Greek kitchen as pastichio and spanakopita, moussaka and loukaniko, souvlaki, gyros, grilled fish, lamb and to finish you off, what else but baklava?

Colonial Plaza, 6108 South Dixie Highway. (407) 582-1666. Inexpensive to moderate. Lunch and dinner.

GREEN OWL
American/Delray Beach

Peter and Suzanne Horn are the proud proprietors of this happy little coffee shop, great for early morning waker-uppers and fun for lunch. Their fresh-brewed soups are excellent, sandwiches heavily stacked and they do good turkey burgers and such daily specials as pot roast, grilled chicken and shepherd's pie, made the British-Irish way—lots of mashed potatoes. There's an army of repeaters elbowed into counter and tables but you never feel like a stranger.

330 East Atlantic Avenue. (407) 272-7766. Inexpensive. Breakfast and lunch.

THE GRILL
Continental/Manalapan

In the best tradition of Cesar Ritz, service here is impeccable, starting with the most professional maitre d' in these parts, Peter Scheuerl, commanding a space that is sheer sophistication, with its beautifully framed paintings on rich, polished wood walls, with intelligently spaced tables and ultra-comfortable chairs and the handsomest of table appointments. We commence our celebration here with house-cured gravlaks, a smoked fish assortment or a confit of duck leg splashed with riesling-raspberry vinaigrette, following up those introductions with a rack of lamb redolent of garlic, grilled grouper and rice noodle cakes with papaya salsa, or the veal scallops smothered with mushrooms and marsala atop a bed of angel hair. The desserts, especially the made-out-back sorbets served in almond waffle baskets with fresh raspberries, are real pleasers and the wine list is awesome. We don't like the word, but how else describe a list with 470 labels, all properly identified with full description and vintage?

The Ritz-Carlton, 100 South Ocean Boulevard. (407) 533-6000. Expensive. Dinner.

THE GROCERY ★
American/Delray Beach

Gourmet glorious with all kinds of specialty foods and a non-stop counter filled with fresh seafood, roasts, beautifully glazed ribs and chickens, cheeses from around the world, a limited selection of wines and a separate gift shop, plus an on-site bakery turning out an outrageous parade of pastries, cakes and above all, cookies. We usually take a few home after lunching informally in the midst of all that plenty a few bites away from the appetite-building display cases. The sirloin burgers and seafood salads are terrific, the sandwiches thickly stacked and they get as fancy as grilled fillets of fresh fish.

Old Harbor Plaza, 1725 South Federal Highway. (407) 243-8016. Inexpensive. Lunch.

GUIDO & PATRICK'S
Continental/Boynton Beach

A highly personal statement in design, service and cheffing, not by Guido & Patrick, but by owners Kathy and Tom Fitzgerald. Tom's grilled shrimp with kiwi salsa, his shrimp and scallop tartlet in a tarragon-spiked mustard sauce, veal with apples in brandy-spiked cream sauce, and fresh Norwegian salmon dusted with macadamia nuts and lemon butter are delivered to the tables with a lot of pride by Kathy and the crew.

Oakland Square, 338 North Congress Avenue. (407) 736-2036. Moderate to expensive. Dinner.

GUPPY'S BAR & GRILL
Seafood/Boca Raton

An incredibly popular place for the locals noon and night serving quality burgers, sandwiches, even one pound T-bones at prices that are out of the 1950s.

45 South Federal Highway. (407) 395-4699. Inexpensive to moderate. Lunch and dinner.

HAMBURGER HEAVEN
American/Palm Beach

Since 1948 a haven for hamburger lovers—they coarse-grind the beef daily and make them to order. But there's more—-come for breakfast as early as 7:00 a.m., or for dinners from November 1 through June, with such fare as beef tenderloin. There's a fine choice of cakes and pies and the prices are hard to believe just a block from Worth Avenue.

314 South County Road. (407) 655-5277. Inexpensive. Breakfast, lunch and dinner.

HAWAIIAN SURFSIDE RESTAURANT
American/South Palm Beach

Dwarfed by the high-rises on both sides, this echo of a bygone era— when Polynesian decor and design was all the rage—is a real sleeper. The oceanfront setting is splendid, the 12-table window-filled room all tropical in furnishings and appointments, and the kitchen turns out a fine parade of good-value-for-the-money meals. Start your day here with a 7 a.m. King Kamehameha plate-filling eye-opener, come back for a salad of freshness kissed with their own made out back dressings, and for dinner to feast on shrimp and scallops given the scampi treatment, a strip sirloin, broiled grouper, halibut or sole, accompanied by an excellent array of vegetables. If you like black bean soup, this is the place to order it.

Palm Beach Hawaiian Ocean Inn, 3550 South Ocean Boulevard. (407) 582-5631. Inexpensive to moderate. Breakfast, lunch and dinner.

HOLIDAY HOUSE
American/Boynton Beach/Lake Worth/Lake Park

These local links of a Florida mini-chain serve some of the best value-for-the-money food to be found on the Gold Coast. It's served cafeteria style with an array of mix and match salad fixins and desserts. They specialize in roast meats fresh from the oven—leg of lamb, Virginia ham, turkey, and two kinds of beef joints, one for the rare crowd and one well done. There are also fish fillets, ground beef patties and all kinds of vegetables and tempting desserts.

710 North Federal Highway, Boynton Beach, (407) 732-6841; 301 North Dixie Highway, Lake Worth, (407) 588-8971; 7201 North Federal Highway, Lake Park, (407) 842-7791. Inexpensive. Lunch and dinner.

HOUSTON'S ★★★
American/Boca Raton

Opened in 1991 in the heart of some of Boca's most expensive business real estate, this latest link in a small chain (the other Florida outpost is in Fort Lauderdale) has been packin' 'em in since the second it opened. The crowds come for the sauteed orange roughy, the grilled fresh fish, the super soups brewed daily, the Caesar, club and sunbelt salads, the platter of fried chicken tenders served with Dijon and hickory sauces, burgers and steaks. The management, supervision and staff performances could serve as case studies in the fine art of running a restaurant.

1900 Executive Center Circle. (407) 998-0500. Moderate to expensive. Lunch and dinner.

IL GIRASOLE
Italian/Delray Beach

Chef-owner Luigi Esposito and maitre'd manager-wife Wilma, provide some interesting departures from the American-Italian norm, an appetizer serving of grilled eggplant terrine with a basil-cheese tomato sauce, entrees of broiled chicken breast with apples, seafood crepes, veal with artichoke hearts in Dijonaise sauce and calves brain sauteed in white wine and lemon sprinkled with capers. A fair selection of wines.

Tropic Square, 1911 South Federal Highway. (407) 272-3566. Expensive. Dinner.

JACKIE'S
American/Delray Beach

Jackie is the chef, partly on view through the pass-through window in what looks like a diner, but is really a rather elegant retreat, one with lace table cloths, fresh plants and, banquet style chairs. Husband Bill is the front man famous for his meatloaf. Entrees include duckling with cranberry sauce, fresh off the boat yellowtail, leg of lamb like none other and nightly specials. The Jazz Sunday brunch is super.

215 North Federal Highway. (407) 243-8029. Moderate to expensive. Dinner and Sunday brunch.

JAPANESE STEAK HOUSE
Japanese/Boca Raton

For the South County bunch that doesn't want to make the drive all the way to Fort Lauderdale for a Benihana fix, this is the place. The sword-wielding chefs—all women, led by Miss Lily, the owner—dazzle with their dexterity before your very eyes, chopping and slicing like Samurai warriors, working over the chunks of prime beef, jumbo shrimp, breast of chicken, mingling it all with bean sprouts, while the shuffling corps de kimonos delivers the see-through soup, simple salad with a sweet dressing, the low-cal dessert.

5751 North Federal Highway. (407) 997-5863. Expensive. Dinner.

JO'S ★★★
French-American/Palm Beach

Rick Kline Jr., the chef in this intimate white latticework little hideaway, does many things right, creating his own kind of Florida fusion cuisine, one that benefits greatly from his several summer sessions with one of the greats, Jean Jacques Rachou of Manhattan's La Cote Basque. From the flowered zucchini filled with shrimp mousse and the boned quail with foie gras and veal sweetbread stuffing, to the rollatines of fresh fish, veal in a morel sauce, and the pastries, all is art. Small but select wine list.

200 Chilean Avenue. (407) 659-6776. Expensive. Dinner.

JUANITA'S
Mexican/Hypoluxo

Hidden in a non-descript structure just north of the Boynton Beach border, Juanita is serving, in a simple setting, a lot of the old standbys fancier places have trouble mastering—tacos and tamales, stuffed chili rellenos, sizzling fajitas and thinly sliced skirt steaks with three alarm sauces.

7768 Federal Highway. (407) 582-9139. Inexpensive. Lunch and dinner.

JOHN G'S
American/Lake Worth

The G stands for Giragos, an Armenian-American who has been at this beachfront location since 1973. It's a great place to start the day—working over an omelet as early as 7 a.m. while watching the sunrise. Come back at lunch for a sirloin burger, fried clams, the corn fritters, which are obviously freshly made, or a platter of lightly-battered fried fillets of fresh fish. The platter is heaped high with straight-from-the-oil fries and a harvest of fresh fruit. It's a bustling, happy place run by the Giragos clan front and back.

Casino Building, 10 South Ocean Boulevard. (407) 585-9860. Inexpensive. Breakfast and lunch.

L'ANJOU
French/Lake Worth

In the here-today-gone-tomorrow whirl of Palm Beach County restaurants, it's always a pleasure to find one that not only survives, but thrives. Since 1975. And they do it by a proper identification of their Lake Worth audience, offering them at budget-pleasing prices a full range of food prepared with French flair in a pleasantly-served setting with tablecloths and French provincial decor. The menu ranges from simple omelets and crepes filled with a variety of savories and sweets, to something as ambitious as lobster thermidor and beef Wellington.

717 Lake Avenue. (407) 582-7666. Moderate. Dinner.

LA CAPANNINA ★
Italian/Palm Beach Gardens

Hidden in a corner of a low-rise shopping center, this tranquil little charmer has been scoring points with us ever since it opened in 1979. Sitting behind the white latticework, soothed by the soft music and enchanted by the floral displays, we commence our meals with an order of angel hair flattened by the diced heart of the tomato enlivened with garlic, basil and a little olive oil, and then work through the veal chop, grilled pompano or fresh yellowtail. Wines are wonderful and the service is very professional and pleasant.

Gardens Square Shoppes, PGA Boulevard andMilitary Trail. (407) 626-4632. Moderate. Lunch and dinner.

LA COSTA D'ORO ★
Italian/Boca Raton

The expansive Cairo clan is encamped here, producing a good many of the American-Italian standbys including buffalo mozzarella with tomato and basil, shrimp scampi, fried calamari, sauteed escarole and broccoli loaded with garlic, to proceed and accompany the saltimboca, veal parmesan, chicken Milanese or scarpariello, the fresh fillets of fish, the Frutta di Mare and Zuppa di Pesce. The dining room is comfortable and happily served, the outside patio terrace is sensational.

21212 St. Andrews Boulevard. (407) 394-0039. Moderate. Dinner.

LA FINESTRA
Continental/Boca Raton

In a sophisticated and intimate evocation of the Parisian Belle Epoque, Serbian chef-owner Antoine Pepaj produces excellent medallions of veal sauteed in sherry with eggplant, fontina, prosciutto and tomatoes; or with chanterelles in a sauce periguex (meaning demi-glaze with diced truffle and essence of truffle) spiked with cognac. We also like the shrimp sauteed with egg and lemon juice enlivened with fresh ginger and the charbroiled filet mignon bearnaise. The pasta combinations are very good and so too are the desserts—the zabaglione, creme brulee and the homemade raspberry ice cream splashed with calvados.

171 East Palmetto Park Road. (407) 392-1838. Expensive. Dinner.

LA PALMA D'ESPANA
Spanish/West Palm Beach

An authentic corner of Spain with a fine assortment of meats and seafood with Ole! tastes. We like the mariscada, the shell fish in green sauce, the baked whole fresh Florida snapper Bilboa style—as good as we ever tasted in Basque country—paella valenciana or marinera. Call ahead for an order of Cordero Lechal Asado a la Castellana, prime baby lamb Castillian style. The staff is eager to showcase their country's cuisine.

401 South Olive Avenue. (407) 659-2160. Moderate. Lunch and dinner.

LA PETITE MAISON ★★★
French/Mediterranean/Boca Raton

Petite indeed! A doll house lovingly looked after by chef-owner Guy Augier and his wife Sylvie, a real charmer. Expatriates from France's Cote d'Azur, they add mightily to the international mix of Boca's restaurant scene, specializing in shrimp salad seduced by a fine garlic cream sauce, garlic-parsley stuffed mussels, escargot with a marvelous spinach au gratin sauce, freshly made pates and terrines, smoked salmon mousse and entrees of grilled chicken in a spicy-peppery sauce Guy calls Mexican, grilled dolphin with tarragon butter, and steak au poivre. Gorgonzola lovers should order the steak surrounded with that mold-freckled gift from the cows in Lombardy, and if you're partial to veal chops, order one here. He adds garlic to the natural juices with great conscience and covers it with a fine mushroom sauce—loaded with morels. The desserts are as delightful as the front porch with all its wicker flower pattern pinks, whites and greens.

366 East Palmetto Park Road. (407) 750-7483. Expensive. Dinner.

Best Hamburger –
Palm Beach

The beauties at Brandyburger, 9804 South Military Trail, Boynton Beach.

LA PINATA
Mexican/Boca Raton

The exiles from Detroit who parked their sombreros in Delray Beach a few years made the move to Boca and more commodious, suitable surrounding. And they added a bit to their bill of fare but still kept the solid standbys—the outstanding gazpacho, sizzling fajitas and the taco-tamale-tostada treats.

3400 North Federal Highway. (407) 750-3588. Inexpensive to moderate. Lunch and dinner.

LA PIAZZA
Italian/Delray Beach

A spacious trattoria that proclaims proudly on its menu that "No salt or MSG is used in our cooking," and offers as appetizer the kind of cream cheese-mushroom-onion-pepper dip with nacho chips non-Italians feature. Dessert of diet-conscious low-fat yogurt rice pudding is also an unusual item to find on an Italian menu, one that does have the old standbys, however, saltimbocca, snapper Francese, shrimp scampi, Suppa di Pesce. The staff is friendly and very eager to satisfy.

Linton International Plaza, 660 Linton Boulevard. (407) 276-5107. Moderate. Lunch and dinner.

LA TRATTORIA
Italian/Boca Raton

Chef Raffaele and front room charmer Francesca are in charge of this happy little enclave of good eating, starting with the complimentary Bruschetta di Pomodoro, the special tasted bread with chopped tomatoes and a light sprinkle of herbs, and the appetizers of spinach pie, mussels marinara. Entrees include angel hair with calamari, veal piccata and veal Sorrentina which Raffaele defines by layering a generous size scallopine with eggplant, prosciutto and provolone, blessing the stack with sherry-spiked lemon sauce. The wine list is OK and the wait staff well informed, thanks to Francesca. We also like the noise level—meaning the overall sense of calm and tranquility.

Village Corner Stores, 6060 Southwest 18th Street. (407) 750-1297. Expensive. Dinner.

Best Hostess-Manager-Owner

Kathy Sellas, the superwoman in charge of the Gazebo Cafe, 4199 North Federal Highway, Boca Raton.

LA TRUC ★
Vietnamese/Boca Raton

Spinoff from a successful parent in Hartford, this is the best-looking Vietnamese restaurant in the state, watched over by chef-owner Binh Duong, who has his own cookbook explaining the finer points of his country's culinary traditions. Here's the perfect place to begin your own education about Tom Tai Chanh, a rice paper roll wrapped around onion-marinated shrimp enlivened by lime juice, sprinkled with finely chopped coriander held at bay with mint; Ga Nuong Chanh, lemon-marinated chicken breast charbroiled on skewers; and the creations called Happy Pancake and Shaking Beef, boredom-breakers of the first rank. Our favorite finisher is the cheesecake.

297 East Palmetto Park Road. (407) 392-4568. Moderate to expensive. Lunch and dinner.

LA VIEILLE MAISON ★★★★
French/Boca Raton

Defines its old house name by rambling through a handsomely land-scaped two-story survivor from the Addison Mizner era, artfully adapted to serve as a stunningly attractive capital of civilized dining. The captains are knowledgeable and experienced, the kitchen highly competent, sometimes brilliant, and the wine list is sensational. The menu is fixed price but you don't have to go the whole ninety yards; you can eliminate certain of the courses and lower your cost.

770 East Palmetto Park Road. (407) 391-6701. Expensive. Dinner.

Best Chinese Restaurant – Palm Beach

Uncle Tai's whose hegira from Manhattan took him through Texas to this opulent temple, 5250 Town Center Circle, Boca Raton.

LA VILLETTA
Italian/Boca Raton

Super chef Maria Mirra-Costanza and super front man Salvatore Sellitto moved north to this little gem from their top-notch Pompano Beach Casa Cacciatore in 1992. Maria designed it with a sure eye for understated elegance, laying out a kitchen that's partially on view when you enter. Together they ascend the summit. The farinaceous fare is worthy of pasta paradise, the marinated-grilled vegetables heart-happy stuff and the Pesce al Naturale, a simply grilled yellowtail expertly deboned tableside by Sal, is a nice way to treat a fresh fish. We also like the respectful way the multi-talented Maria handles the veal, especially the Vitello Martherita, sauteed with fresh tomatoes and basil with a light cover of mozzarella, and the Bocconcini alla Villeta, a rolled scallopine layered with mushrooms mozzarella and spinach in the lightest of cream sauces. The desserts—cheese torte and tiramisu are my favorites—are also special and the wine list is excellent—let Sal guide you.

4351 North Federal Highway. (407) 362-8403. Expensive. Dinner.

LAI LAI
Chinese/Boca Raton

Following up their success with the first Lai Lai in Plantation, at Mercede Arcade, these expansion-minded Chinese followed the migration and the money north. Here they serve the same kind of Cantonese and Mandarin specialties as the parent. That means dim sum dumplings fried or steamed, a better than average hot and sour soup, excellent mu-shu pork and a variety of seafood selections—we like the shrimp-scallop combination in a light, creamy, comforting sauce.

Del-Mar Shopping Village, Powerline and Palmetto Park Road. (407) 395-2866. Moderate. Lunch and dinner.

LE MONEGASQUE   ★★
French/Palm Beach

Started in 1974 by veteran New York restaurateur Aldo Riniero who turned over the reins 14 years later to Regine and Raymond Maistri. They have maintained the standards, serving superb salmon in a sorrel sauce, Florida version of bouillabaisse, Dover sole, frog legs, rack of lamb and veal chops all prepared in the French manner. Hidden away on the ground floor of a condominium which has rigid sign restrictions and does not allow advertising, this little slice of Monaco is not easy to find but well worth the effort.

The President, 2505 South Ocean Boulevard. (407) 585-0071. Expensive. Dinner. Closed July through September.

LE VIEUX PARIS
French/Boca Raton

Totally captivating little cafe that in spirit and sustenance is reminiscent of something simple on a side street in Paris, but in setting this is Vieux Boca, for there are grand photo blowups on the wall detailing the boom and bust Addison Mizner background of Boca. Nothing sensational is served here to write Lyon about, but the food is solid, simple, consistent.

170 West Camino Real. (407) 368-7910. Moderate. Dinner.

LITTLE BRAU HAUS
German/Lake Worth

Little is indeed the right word. But the hearts of the owners are big and the German specialties very good. But not everything on the menu is kraut, wurst and sauerbraten. We had some of the best ever corned beef and cabbage on St. Patrick's Day.

#17, South J Avenue. (407) 585-3186. Moderate. Dinner. Closed mid-August to mid-October. No credit cards.

THE LITTLE MERMAID ★★
Danish/Delray Beach

Danophiles take note! This is Hans Christian Andersen with such Fairy Tale Dinners as The Emperor's New Suit (veal cutlet with anchovies, capers and horseradish), The Phoenix Bird (baked chicken breast with raspberry cream sauce), Little Claus and Big Claus (veal meatballs with red cabbage and white potatoes), and so on. Good food, fun, and the dedication of the owners, Gail and John Isaksen, who's certainly not the melancholy Dane. Not when he makes such perfect frikedelle, those Marvelous little veal meatballs, and finishes off with one of those Danish whipped cream cakes.

505 Northeast 5th Avenue. (407) 276-6900. Moderate. Dinner.

LONE STARR STEAKS
American/Delray Beach

A quintessential Texas steak house with all kinds of western memorabilia, including a collection of "jackalopes" and the horns from the prize bull who starred in the western centennial film. The staff is unusually friendly, the steaks better than the Outback's and the chili is marvelous.

5130 Linton Boulevard. (407) 499-3130. Moderate. Lunch and dinner.

LUCILLE & OTLEY'S
American/Boynton

What started more than a half century ago as a pie shop has turned into a beloved institution filled with loyal fans, senior citizens in the main, who like the speedy service, the well-lighted tables, the no-nonsense menu featuring roast lamb and ham—served with pineapple of course—fillets of fish, mashed potatoes and two, maybe three vegetables. Pies are still a highlight. We like the banana cream as well as the hallmark lemon meringue.

1021 South Federal Highway. (407) 732-5930. Moderate to expensive. Dinner and Sunday brunch. Closed June through October.

LUNAS
American/Delray Beach

What we like most about this moonscape are the indoor-outdoor location in a pretty little plaza, the friendliness of the staff, the class act at the piano, and the luncheon buffets, one of the best value-for-the-money spreads for miles around. After a period of inconsistency, the kitchen straightened itself out and is again showing consistency in its preparation of fish fillets, shrimp and scallops, veal and beef.

Atlantic Plaza, 777 East Atlantic Avenue. (407) 276-6279. Moderate to expensive. Lunch and dinner.

MANDARIN VALLEY
Chinese/Boca Raton

We first explored the Mandarin Valley in Fort Lauderdale and were so impressed at the talents of the chefs and the determination of management to go far, far beyond the chop suey glop that we returned. Again and again. When they established this mission in a much higher rent district, we did some more exploring and found the levels of performance as high as the first. In a much more attractive setting, with a knockout jade wall mural and a black-suited staff well suited to the tastes of west Boca.

21073 Jog Road. (407) 487-9966. Moderate to expensive. Lunch and dinner

MARCEL'S
French/Boca Raton

A pretty restaurant with the warmth of something special in the French provinces, watched over by Marcel Wortman who has had two other restaurants in Boca. His private party rooms are very popular, but we go for the noontime shrimp with basil-blessed tomatoes, chicken breast tarragon, chopped tenderloin with a sauce of red wine-shallots or Madagascar green peppercorns. For dinner we start with the made out back terrine of pheasant with pistachios and onion confiture, or the salad of warm sea scallops, followed by duckling, salmon fillet with morels, or the veal medallion with wild mushrooms in a champagne sauce. The desserts, especially the sorbets and floating island, are excellent.

One South Ocean Boulevard (A1A). (407) 362-9911. Expensive. Lunch and dinner.

MARCELLO'S LA SIRENA
Italian/West Palm Beach

The intimate domain of Marcello Fiorentino who in years past cut quite a swath across the Palm Beach restaurant whirl but is now content with a more manageable arena of action. When we dine here, amidst a surprising level of formality considering the size of the place and the neighborhood, we put ourselves in his able hands, enjoying every minute of his monologue while we decide what to order.

6316 South Dixie Highway. (407) 585-3128. Expensive. Dinner.

MARGARITA Y AMIGAS
Mexican/West Palm Beach

Since 1981 this spacious cantina with an oversize bar and many privacy-possible booths has been perfecting and polishing its act, preparing excellent Spanish-Mexican rice, nachos, mucho grande burros and fabulously flavorful chicken dishes along with the usual taco-tamale-tostada stuff.

2030 Palm Beach Lakes Boulevard. (407) 684-7788. Inexpensive to moderate. Lunch and dinner.

MARGIE'S CAFE
American/Boca Raton

Here's a coffee shop supreme, run by an American-American family. Harry is the manager and money man; wife Louise is the ever-smiling, gracious Mary Poppins (as Harry refers to her); and sister Margie is the one with all the treasured family recipes, the kitchen guru in charge of the younger generation out back. The breakfasts here are bountiful—you'll wait on the weekends—and the lunches memorable—in a Margie kind of way. That means you have to order her American butter roll, Katah or the Choreg roll freckled with sesame seeds. Either one is a marvelous friend for the salads. Other treats are the half-pound burgers, the fresh greens criss-crossed with strips of broiled chicken and the L'Joons, a thin round crust spread with a finely minced meat mixture lightly spiced before baking. Oh yes, there is a Slim & Trim side of the menu but who wants to look there when there's so much great flavor elsewhere?

1840 North Dixie Highway. (407) 368-7270. Inexpensive to moderate. Breakfast and lunch.

MARIO'S
Italian/Boca Raton

Subs, hoagies, pizzas and a noon-time buffet are the highlights of this popular trattoria. The garlic rolls are wonderful, and they serve tons of veal, schools of seafood, pasta in every which way. The setting is good enough to have won a Florida Designer Guild award. The crowds really congregate here, especially during the season but the prices are right and the lunch buffets bountiful enough to bust your belt.

Glades Plaza, 2200 Glades Road. (407) 392-5595. Moderate. Lunch and dinner.

MATSU-SUSHI
Japanese/Boca Raton

Sushi and sashimi headquarters for west Boca dwellers who have learned the joys of dipping beautifully assembled rice rolls into soy sauce with the zing of that hotter-than-hot horseradish called wasabi. Or biting into a crisp tempura crust surrounding shrimp and veggies as prelude to something from the teppan grill.

19605-A State Road 7. (407) 487-0693. Moderate. Lunch and dinner.

MAXALUNA TUSCAN GRILL ★★
Italian/Boca Raton

High Tech design, kitchen-on-view, Tuscan wood-burning grill, up-front bar. There are now five others, and Cal-Italia cafes all over the Gold Coast. In season there's usually a jamup for seats, especially for those who don't want to be too close to the cooking or in other high-decibel sections. What to eat and drink? Any of the specials including the wines.

Crocker Center, 21150 Military Trail. (407) 391-7177. Expensive. Lunch and dinner.

MAX'S GRILLE ★★
American/Boca Raton

A bustling, noisy, indoor-outdoor grill designed in the best LA Cafe manner and featuring innovative cuisine of the first order.

Mizner Park, 404 Plaza Real. (407) 368-0080. Moderate to expensive. Lunch and dinner.

MELTING POT
Fondue/Boca Raton

Do you fondue? Dipping chunks of bread into bubbling cheese, pieces of meat in vegetable oil, fruit in melted, hot chocolate? Then this is the place for you.

5455 North Federal Highway, Suite A. (407) 997-7472. Moderate. Dinner.

MONTY'S
Seafood/Boca Raton

A northern mission from the much more famous Monty's in Miami's Coconut Grove, this too specializes in stone crab claws with all-you-can-eat servings at good prices. And they're served all year long because when the Florida season is shut down (May 15—October15), Monty's flies in the claws from South America. You can also get fried shrimp, fresh Florida fillets of grouper, dolphin, snapper, good garlic and rosemary-infused grilled chicken breast and a fine rib eye steak with horseradish sauce.

2300 Executive Center Drive. (407) 994-5626. Expensive. Dinner.

MORADA BAR & GRILL
American/Boca Raton

Build up an appetite by watching the kitchen at work through giant windows by the entrance and then start an evening with wild mushroom quesadilla, or beef carpaccio with white truffles, locatelli, pinenuts, roasted peppers and aioli. Move on to smoked duck ravioli, porcini linguine, roasted rack of lamb, sesame-charred tuna or a veal chop with three peppercorn—burgundy sauce. That is, if any of the above is on the menu. It changes regularly and there's always a good number of nightly specials.

Crocker Center, 5100 Town Center Circle, Suite 100. (407) 395-0805. Expensive. Dinner.

Best Sorbet Presentation

The silver-crowned cart at La Vieille Maison, 770 East Palmetto Park Road, Boca Raton.

MORTON'S OF CHICAGO ★
American/West Palm Beach

If you're a heartlander from the Windy City you know the reputation of Morton's, a premier steak house which of late has been bitten by the clone-chain bug. The setting here is strictly downtown with an eye-riveting display of produce and the kitchen on view. Don't think about the appetizers or the desserts; go directly to the porterhouse, the sirloins and filet mignons, as displayed by the waiter who brings the raw material to the table for show and tell. And remember anything else you want on the plate with all that prime beef is going to be extra, though excellent, whether you order a baked potato, steamed asparagus or broccoli.

Phillips Point, 777 South Flagler Drive. (407) 835-9664. Expensive. Dinner.

MUER'S SEAFOOD
Seafood/Boca Raton

The original Joe Muer Seafood in Detroit, opened at 2000 Gratiot Avenue in the 1920s. The emphasis there as well as here was all seafood, and it's prepared in the same manner as the Charley's Crab outlets in Florida and elsewhere. The setting is formal but friendly and the wine list is California select. And they're still serving the complimentary beans and bread to launch you on your evening of seafood adventure.

6450 North Federal Highway. (407) 997-6688. Expensive. Lunch and dinner.

NANDO'S
Italian/Palm Beach

The second generation, and maybe the third as well, is now on the scene in this beloved landmark creating a comfort zone with a piano lounge up front and a menu loaded with the full-blown features of the kitchen. Our meals here usually kick off with shrimp scampi, move into the farinaceous area, preferably something with angel hair, and climax with veal piccata or saltimbocca.

221 Royal Palm Way. (407) 655-3031. Expensive. Dinner. Jackets suggested. Closed month of July.

NARCISSUS
American/West Palm Beach

With jazz every evening and during the Sunday brunch, this is a popular watering hole, wonderful in the right season with its sidewalk tables. We come for the noontime sandwiches, especially the one with Maryland crab cake, and such super soups as their brew blending artichokes and mushrooms so masterfully. There are seven pastabilities including those mingling scallops and shrimp scampi, wild mushrooms and grilled chicken along with very good North Atlantic salmon and marinated lamb chops.

200 Clematis Street. (407) 659-1888. Moderate. Lunch, dinner and Sunday brunch.

NICK'S DINER
American/West Palm Beach

When you're roaring along I-95 in West Palm Beach and feel an attack of the kind of hungries only a diner can cure, take the Okeechobee exit west and immediately look for what Nick boasts is "A 50s Experience." He's got the neon, soda fountain, glass bricks, Elvis and James Dean memorabilia to prove it; he serves all the good stuff—chili crowned with cheddar and chopped onions, great burgers, Greek salads and gyros, and 22 Deluxe Dinners served with soup, mashed potatoes, vegetable and rolls at pocketbook-pleasing prices.

Palm Beach Market Place, 1900 Okeechobee Boulevard. (407) 471-3155. Inexpensive. Breakfast, lunch and dinner.

NICK'S ITALIAN FISHERY
Seafood/Boca Raton

Chef-owner Nick Bimonte exploded on the scene in 1990 with this smashing success in some of Boca's most uppity of upscale office center buildings. Framed by a piano lounge up front, and a large display kitchen along the back, it indeed specializes in seafood, but not to be overlooked are the warm cheese-garlic slabs of bread, the pasta, and the terrific desserts. Noontime buffets are real budget-conscious spreads, and the serving staff responds well to the setting and challenges met by the kitchen.

One Boca Place, Glades Road and I-95. (407) 994-2201. Expensive. Lunch and dinner.

THE OCEAN GRILL
Seafood/Manalapan

In the ultra posh surroundings of Manalapan, this indoor-outdoor cafe provides a fine setting for snacking and supping, lunching and munching. The inside dining room with its comfortable banquettes and soft colors has an inviting bar—as all kind of celebrities have discovered. We like the noontime salads and the dramatic evening presentations of grilled duck breast—from Indiana not Long Island— dill-encrusted Atlantic salmon, preceded by crab quesadillas criss-crossed with creamy white ribbons, or the smoked salmon served with the requisite toast points.

Plaza Del Mar, A1A & Ocean Avenue. (407) 547-7101. Moderate. Lunch and dinner.

ORCHIDS OF SIAM
Thai/West Palm Beach

Orchids to this Thai temple with one of the longest-running menus this side of the Land of Smiles—-no fewer than 74 individual items, plus special luncheon and early bird dinner savings. The most modest dining-out budgets have ample room to maneuver, from the starter courses of soups, do-it-yourself satay, or the spicy shrimp, to the appetite-satisfying curried meats and seafood held at bay with coconut milk.

3027 Forest Hill Boulevard. (407) 969-2444. Moderate. Lunch and dinner.

ORIENTAL DRAGON
Chinese/Boca Raton

Large and well-lighted place with amiable, knowledgeable service, and one of those just-won't-quit menus with all kinds of combinations and crossovers. We start with the steamed dumplings and then concentrate on the Cantonese chicken or Szechuan shrimp, hoping that the message in our fortune cookie will explain how so many Chinese restaurants can survive in South Florida.

1279 West Palmetto Park Road. (407) 392-6688. Inexpensive to moderate. Lunch and dinner.

OUTBACK STEAKHOUSE
American/Boca Raton/West Palm Beach

Palm Beach County links in the latest rage creating a basic meat and potatoes kind of place, one with fair prices for quality food, well-supervised service, a cutsey menu with Boomerang Burgers, Ribs on the Barbie and Jackeroo chops.

Village Pointe, 6030 Southwest 18th Street, Boca Raton, (407) 338-6283; 901 Village Boulevard, West Palm Beach, (407) 683-1011. Moderate. Dinner.

OXLEY'S SEAFOOD RESTAURANT
Seafood/Boca Raton

Ever since architect-entrepreneur Addison Mizner dreamt up Boca Raton back in the 1920s, polo has been an integral part of the vision. And it certainly is today, with a fine stadium for watching the ponies, with lushly green practice fields, and this splendid polo-theme restaurant underneath the grandstand. Seafood is their specialty, and it's as thoroughbred as the horses pounding the turf. We start here with one of their chowders or bisques, then shift gears to grilled swordfish or one of those lusciously pink fillets of fresh salmon from the Norwegian fjords.

Royal Palm Polo Grounds, 6300 Clint Moore Road. (407) 994-1883. Moderate to expensive. Dinner. Closed August through September.

PAMPERED PALATE CAFE AND BISTRO
Continental/Boca Raton

What a location—Bloomie's on one flank and Saks on the other, in the up-up-scale surroundings of Town Center. Celebrate that catch off the sale rack with a large seafood salad, some made-out-back pasta, grilled chicken or steaks, and in the proper season, twin Maine lobsters at some of the best prices in South Florida. The cafe ambiance is welcoming and the piano music at dinner soothing. Informal cafe atmosphere, live entertainment. Moderate. Lunch and dinner.

Town Center Mall, Between Bloomingdales and Saks. (407) 391-8211. Moderate. Lunch and dinner.

PAN-AMERICAN
Cuban/West Palm Beach

For anyone interested in stretching the dining-out dollar, this is definitely a stop on the budget trail. Owned and operated by partners Cileda Pino, a Cuban, and Ramon Mendez, a Puerto Rican, it is similar in style and spirit to any number of storefront feederies found all over Miami's little Havana—and now popping up in Broward and Palm Beach counties. Headliners are such old friends as black bean soup, Cuban sandwiches, tamales, shrimp creole, fried plantains, arroz con pollo.

North Dixie Highway and 10th Street. (407) 833-6918. Inexpensive. Lunch and dinner. Closed June through September for dinner.

PANCHO VILLA
Mexican/Colombian/Lake Worth

The Cardonas from Colombia run this out of the way storefront with specialities from their homeland and Mexican marvels that are far better than the run of the molino stuff. We always start our eating adventure here with some of those wonderful crescents of beef and potato mashed into corn meal and called empanadas, followed by Sancocho Stew, a peasant kind of brew with chunks of chicken, potato, plantains and yuca. Or go not so far South of the Border and order chile rellenos, chimichangas or the hot tamales.

Mil-Lake Plaza, 4663 Lake Worth Road. (407) 964-1112. Inexpensive. Lunch and dinner.

PASTA MARKET CAFE
Italian/Boca Raton

Penny and Ken Kuzmenko moved to this attractive location in 1991, expanding considerably their space and guest list and supervising a kitchen that does all things right transferring their kitchen's magic way with pasta in all its forms. Beyond the farinaceous fare is to be found veal pizzaiola, grilled swordfish au poivre, chicken breast with pecan sauce. But save space for Penny's unbelievably rich desserts. The carrot cake is fabulous and her brownie has little competition in the high cal department. Another advantage—and it's a stunner—are the revolving displays of Haitian Art. The gallery is around the corner.

1600 North Federal Highway. (407) 392-3782. Moderate to expensive. Lunch and dinner.

PETE'S
American/Boca Raton

Owner-operator Pete Boinis is really going for the gold in this multi-level, many-splendour and highly stylized supper club with live bands, dance floor, giant bar, walls of windows overlooking an attractively land-scaped pond. For lunch we like the fried cheese ravioli, the super gener-ous salads and heart smart selections; for dinner the superlative caviar-dolloped vichyssoise, broccoli-cheddar or wild berry soup, followed by chicken marsala lobster thermidor, veal oscar or poached salmon with lemon butter. Excellent wine list and very friendly, solitious service.

Arvida Parkway, 7940 Glades Road. (407) 487-1600. Moderate to expensive. Lunch and dinner.

PINE GARDEN
Chinese/Boca Raton

Hold the beef, forget the fish and cut out chicken! This is a vegetarian's paradise, with no MSG but with vegetable oil, and 37 different meatless selections, all served with excellent brown rice. Dubious? Order the sea-weed-bean curd soup, vegetable spring roll, pan-fried noodles with thick slices of eggplant substituting for fish, the Chinese root vegetable, taro, taking the place of pork in the sweet and sour pork classic and the wheat gluten Sang Kan spiked with Szechuan peppers tasting like chicken make you forget that you're not eating the real thing. Cashews, garlic, lemon, ginger, peppers are all used in abundance by a chef who has mastered the fine art of Chinese vegetarianism. Oh yes, they have a regular menu too.

1668 North Federal Highway. (407) 395-7534. Moderate. Lunch and dinner. Closed August.

PLAZA CAFE
Continental/Delray Beach

Chef-owner David Zucker is the enthusiastic chef-owner and he's assem-bled a professional staff to serve his nightly specials predicated on the market supply and his own need to break the routine. Rely on his recom-mendations or those of the captain-waiter-maitre d', but make sure that if David is doing duck that day, you order it.

Boca Ray Plaza, 4900 Linton Boulevard. (407) 499-5311. Moderate to expensive. Lunch and dinner.

PORTO BELLO
Italian/Boynton Beach

A fine family storefront with a split personality—-stark pizza take-out space on one side, a trattoria on the other. The pizza is good, but so too are the pasta dishes, the cutlet Milanese and chicken cacciatore. Mama is always on the premises, keeping a watchful eye on the operation, fussing around the corners to make sure this porto is always bella.

Boynton Trail Center, 9770 South Military Trail.(407) 738-5600. Moderate. Lunch and dinner.

PORTOFINO
Italian/Singer Island

On the municipal beach with an outside service counter, an inside luncheon buffet, and a menu that goes on and on, starting with pizzas—trenchermen swear by their let-it-all-hang-on thickly layered house special. We like the family feeling, the proud display of the ancestry at the entrance, the made-to-order veal and pasta dishes.

Ocean Mall, 2447 Ocean Boulevard. (407) 844-8411. Moderate. Breakfast, lunch and dinner.

PREZZO
Italian/Boca Raton

Patio-terrace overlooking Pete's pond, baci court, wood-burning ovens, pasta and bread makers on view, smiling staff and serious supervision, a decor and design that is very much today. All that by way of introduction to a routine-smashing menu—the kind of pastas and pizzas developed in LA Cafes: oak-grilled salmon, veal cutlets, sauteed chicken and spinach. Good wines. The success here led to the cloning of other links in a budding mini-chain in Kendall and Aventura, both in Dade County.

Arivda Parkway Center, 7820 Glades Road. (407) 451-2800. Moderate. Lunch and dinner.

Best Family Act Italian Style

The happy crew at Renzo's, 5999 North Federal Highway, Boca Raton.

PRONTI'S ITALIAN KITCHEN
Italian/Lake Park

There has been such an incredible proliferation of Italian restaurants in recent years, spanning the gamut from the simplest mom and pop pizzeria to over-cute trattoria and grand ristorante, that we sometimes fear we will be swept away by a tidal wave of marinara sauce (clutching a Chinese red-tassel lantern of course). This place was well-established before the onslaught, opening in 1972 and steadily building a loyal corps of customers who like the from-scratch approach to the seafood and veal preparations, the homemade salad dressings, the friendliness of the staff.

1440 10th Street. (407) 842-3457. Inexpensive to moderate. Dinner.

Best Hot and Sour Soup

The flawless counterbalancing act at Feng Lin, Harbor Plaza, 1725 South Federal Highway, Delray Beach.

RAFFAELLO'S   ★★
Italian/Boca Raton

In 1992 Raffaello moored a few feet closer to the ocean by moving from his former location to this Addison Mizner era home, one that's been attractively transformed into intimate dining rooms, served by a formally-clad, skilled staff. Best space for me is the Wine Room where a half dozen guests can sit in quiet comfort, surveying the cellar and deciding what to order. There are always nightly specials along with the standbys—Caesar salad mixed for two tableside, smoked Norwegian salmon reposing on radicchio and pastry pockets of snails with spinach and a red pepper sauce. After those good beginnings, it's time for veal scallops sauteed with capers and lemon; rack of lamb with a load of garlic plus a splash of balsamic vinaigrette and a restrained sprinkling of herbs; Dover sole or the Coniglop con Broccoli Rape, rabbit sauteed with that strong breed of Italian broccoli. The wine list is a good one albeit a bit steep in price.

725 East Palmetto Park Road. (407) 392-4855. Expensive. Dinner.

RAINBOW ROOM
American/Boca Raton

The Tremaine family, led by John and Alberta, "Bert", took over this snazzy supper club from Ciro's Pomodoro in 1993 and they've installed a new menu, one that promises "each menu selection has no more total percent of calories from fat than a stewed, skinless chicken leg." It's part of their "bodyfat management" concept and is good news when faced with such choices as pasta and Maine lobster, seafood and steaks. There's no Nautilus gear on the premises, but there is a large dance floor with lively bands, so you can burn off more calories in between bites.

1499 West Palmetto Park Road. (407) 395-9115. Expensive. Dinner.

RAINDANCER STEAK HOUSE ★★
American/West Palm Beach

Any restaurant that has survived—no, make that thrived—since 1975 in one of the most competitive markets in the world must be doing something right. Here they do everything right, from the supervision of a professional, pleasant staff to the maintenance of a non-threatening pub-club setting, from crowned-with-cheese French onion soup to the apple pie with cinnamon ice cream. In between, order the fresh fish of the day, one of the several surf and turf combinations or the beef. This is after all a steak house and their sirloins and filets are superb. So too is the privilege of having a dozen wines available by the glass from a pretty good list.

2300 Palm Beach Lakes Boulevard. (407) 684-2810. Moderate to expensive. Dinner.

THE RED LION
British/Boynton Beach

Since 1983 this strip mall pub has been South County's headquarters for bangers and mash, shepherd pies, curried chicken, Scotch eggs, and other pub grub, the kind found in hundreds if not thousands of pubs throughout the British Isles.

Plaza, 10114 South Military Trail. (407) 737-0434. Inexpensive to moderate. Dinner. No credit cards.

RENATO'S
Italian/Palm Beach

Tucked into the most important piece of Worth Avenue real estate, the courtyard of the mirador-crowned apartments and offices built by Alladin-architect Addison Mizner, this well-served outpost of northern Italian cuisine is an ideal place to discuss that past and celebrate the present with a veal chop and wild mushrooms, some jump in the mouth saltimbocca, complimented with a fine Italian red, and climaxed with raspberry mousse or a fruit tart.

87 Via Mizner. (407) 655-9752. Expensive. Dinner.

RENZO'S OF BOCA
Italian/Boca Raton

★★★

An intensely personal achievement by the Renzo clan who devote all their energies and experiences to make absolutely certain their guests leave totally contented, after having one of their 16 pastas-penne with vodka or puttanesca sauce are our favorites—seven shrimp entrees and a like number of chicken, or such house specials as "Linguini Frutti di Mare", veal Sorrentino surrounded by eggplant, mozzarella and prosciutto; or angel hair tangled with shrimp and scallops flattered with cognac-spiked cream sauce and a touch of marinara.

5999 North Federal Highway. (407) 994-3495. Moderate to expensive. Lunch and dinner.

Best Sidewalk Cafe

Chuck and Harold's where you watch the sheer set pass in review, 207 Royal Poinciana Way, Palm Beach.

THE RESTAURANT ★★★★
American/Palm Beach

The understatement of the name typifies the subtle elegance of the room with stunning table appointments and the genius of executive chef Hubert des Marais, who mixes and matches the cuisines of the Caribbean and the Southeast with great finesse and flourish. He changes the menu weekly spotlighting such stunners as barbecued veal loin, wood-grilled beef with a guava-tamarind salute, kumquat-embraced pheasant, salmon blessed by habanero butter with a touch of mango, yellowtail with a smoky orange sauce. Good wine list and splendid service. He imports his organically grown greens and mushrooms from as far afield as Oregon, and grows his own herbs and citrus. It all combines to make this the best hotel dining room in the county.

The Ocean Grand, 2800 South Ocean Boulevard. (407) 582-2800. Expensive. Dinner.

THE RIVERHOUSE
Seafood/Palm Beach Gardens

Overlooking a strategic section of the Intracoastal, this superbly served multi-level retreat has a straight-forward menu, starters of shrimp cocktail, smoked kingfish and New England clam chowder, entrees of grilled salmon with dill sauce, grouper in the pouch with spinach, and prime rib. The second deck has tablecloths and a bit more class.

Soverel Marina, 2373 PGA Boulevard. (407) 694-1188. Expensive. Dinner.

RIZZO'S
Italian/Boca Raton

Boca's oldest restaurant, established in 1965 and still featuring, the same kind of specialties—cheese ravioli, baked lasagna, eggplant parmesan and fettuccine Alfredo. We usually wind up ordering the poached salmon with cold dill sauce, mussels marinara on linguine, or shrimp Francese, always accompanied by the bowl of cole slaw brought to the table family style.

5990 North Federal Highway. (407) 997-8080. Moderate to expensive. Lunch and dinner.

ROD & GUN
American/Delray Beach

Housed in a unique building that looks as though it was magically transported en toto from a hunting estate in the Carolina hills, this escape is the place for such adventurous, blah-breaking fare as gator tail and venison, but they also serve a pretty good wiernerschnitzel a la Holstein, stuffed lobster, prime rib and Norwegian salmon.

4285 West Atlantic Avenue. (407) 496-2150. Moderate to expensive. Dinner.

ROSIE'S KEY WEST GRILL
American/Delray Beach/Lake Worth/
West Palm Beach

I celebrated 1992's St. Patrick's Day by eating some of the best corned beef and cabbage at the newly opened Delray Beach link in this mini-chain. In later visits, I stretched my mouth over a half-pound charbroiled chuck burger, chicken tenders and Cajunized shrimp, and one of the 11 "Rosie's Famous Sandwiches,"—the steak is my favorite. The setting is Key West and the staff lively and very friendly.

1524 South Federal Highway, Delray Beach, (407) 274-7071; 612 Lake Avenue, Lake Worth, (407) 582-1330; 4068 Forest Hill Boulevard, West Palm Beach, (407) 966-0815. Inexpensive. Lunch and dinner.

ROYAL CHEF
Chinese/West Palm Beach

Sheng Su, otherwise known as Peter Su, is the chef-owner in this excellent restaurant, one that would never use MSG, over-salt, over-spice or overwhelm with steam table glop. The former chef at the Taiwanese Embassy in Washington, Su is a highly articulate, enthusiastic artist who does sensational dim sum dumplings and crystal shrimp. General Su's chicken is also a winner.

Target Plaza, 1969 South Military Trail. (407) 964-3229. Moderate. Lunch and dinner.

THE ROYAL GREEK
Greek/West Palm Beach

Uncomplicated taverna Florida style with a few reminders of the Old Country and more tasteful reminders on the menu: lamb shank with rice pilaf, moussaka, fish grilled Greek style, shrimp Mykonos. Forget the baklava and zero in on something from the revolving pastry case—made by these royal Greeks.

7100 South Dixie Highway. (407) 585-7292. Inexpensive to moderate. Breakfast, lunch and dinner.

SAGAMI ★
Japanese/West Palm Beach

A northern offshot from the same folks who scored so successfully with Sagamis in Broward County this one is in an enclave of elegance and features the same high level of sushi and sushimi artistry at the longest sushi bar in South Florida, a wonderful place to experiment with everything from abalone to sea urchin and tuna belly. Swiftly woked tempura, carefully prepared sukiyaki and various combination possibilities complete the production along with a red bean ice cream.

871 Village Boulevard. (407) 683-4600. Moderate. Lunch and dinner.

SAIGON GARDEN
Vietnamese/Lantana

Here is a fine place to be introduced to the intricacies of Banh Xeo, Ga Xao Lan, Bo Luc Lac, Ca Hap, and Chao Tom, which spells Happy Pancake with shrimp, mushrooms, onion and beansprouts; chicken with curry and coconut milk; filet mignon with garlic and watercress; steamed fish and a shrimp pate worked into sugar cane stalks and charbroiled. Try it! You'll like it!

Island Club Shoppes, 3618 Lantana Road. (407) 641-3138. Inexpensive to moderate. Lunch and dinner.

SAIGON PALACE
Vietnamese/Lake Worth

In addition to the pleasures of the Vietnamese kitchen, this palace on the weekends features Vietnamese music on the 16-string harp. So while you're laughing with your Happy Pancake, or bouncing with your Shaking Beef, you can learn a little more about the culture and charm of a much-troubled land, asking all the while for explanations of the various specialties on the menu.

Mil-Lake Plaza, 4631 Lake Worth Road. (407) 439-1015. Inexpensive to moderate. Lunch and dinner.

Best Chili

Huck Finn would love the version served at Tom Sawyer's, 1759 Northwest Second Avenue, Boca Raton.

SAIL INN
American/Delray Beach

Thimble-size tavern and watering hole since 1953 for a disparate collection of fans and friends. The bar dominates, but there are a few tables for lunching and munching on excellent chili, the house burger with bacon and provolone, fish 'n' chips and thickly-stacked sandwiches. The Rueben is terrific.

657 Northeast 8th Street. (407) 276-5147. Inexpensive. Lunch and dinner.

ST. HONORE' ★★★★
French/Palm Beach Gardens

When I succeed in getting the Michelin reviewing team to Palm Beach County, this will be the first stop—and if they don't give it top ranking, I'll send them packing. In a word, St. Honore' is super. An instant transport to something very special in France, it always reminds me of one of the great restaurants in champagne country, in Reims. But then chef-partner Alain Jorand is a pupil of Boyer whose two restaurants there are among my favorites in the world. Jorand does everything well but it's best to be charmed by his partner Pierre Boutiron, the quintessential French maitre d', who will guide you to a handsomely appointed table indoors, where there's a fireplace cheerily crackling on cold nights, or out on the patio. He then will guide you through the menu with such tantalizers as roast squab with a spicy, caramelized sauce and fried celery root; beef tenderloin in raisin sauce. Magret of duckling treated to a thyme-honey sauce and lobster in a variety of salutatious-sauternes are my favorites. Remember to conclude with the St. Honore' cakes; after all, the restaurant is named for the patron saint of bakers and patissiers.

Harbour Village, 2401 PGA Boulevard. (407) 627-9099. Expensive. Dinner. Lunch November through May.

ST. TROPEZ
French/Boca Raton

The culinary creations of Egyptian chef-owner Esam Hamdy are imitative rather than original, but he's determined that his poached salmon, grilled swordfish, rack of lamb, duckling au poivre, and all else that comes out of his kitchen will be better than anyone else can offer. And out front the charm of Cairo-born wife Sonia, ensures there's a high level of sophistication and solicitude.

7000 West Camino Real. (407) 368-4119. Expensive. Lunch and dinner.

SANDE'S
American/Delray Beach

A coffee shop from the pre-boom Delray days, one with a counter and cozy booths usually occupied from dawn to dusk, with lots of repeat customers. The morning omelets provide stoking for the day, the afternoon burgers and sandwiches are all made to order and the dinners are built around a variety of diner-type solid offerings.

1717 North Federal Highway. (407) 272-9104. Inexpensive. Breakfast, lunch and dinner.

SAPORI
Italian/Boca Raton

The name means "tastes" and it was chosen with high hopes by the Pindo brothers, chef Marco and maitre d' Raffelle, to describe their little cafe with a cross-cultural menu. Couscous, the national dish of the Mahgreb, is used to stuff mussels, wonton skins to wrap escargots, and ginger to great advantage for a swordfish Sapori sauce, blended perfectly, if not platonically, with balsamic vinegar, garlic and honey. The filet mignon filled with a bit of bourbon and prosciutto splashed with Madeira, the garlic-roasted chicken and Brodetto Di Pesce, a stew pot harvest from the deep, are also tastes that are terrific.

Royal Palm Plaza No. 99, 301 Via De Palmes. (407) 367-9779. Moderate to expensive. Lunch and dinner.

SAY'S THAI CUISINE
Thai-Laotian/Boca Raton

Manorak and Viengsay Luangkhot have introduced to Palm Beach County Laotian cuisine—salads made from green papaya, barbecued chicken marinated with lemon grass and zapped with a tomato base hot sauce, lapp, a mass of greenery mingled with highly-spiced, peppered beef. Necessary accompaniment is the unique sticky rice, which makes a repeat appearance as dessert when covered with coconut milk, sliced mango and sesame. Then there's all the Thai specialties, from Mee Krob and Nam Sod to Siam duck, basil frog legs, and the green, masman, panang and red curry dishes.

Glades Plaza, Suite 901, 2200 West Glades Road. (407) 393-0341. Moderate to expensive. Lunch and dinner.

SCOREBOARD
American/Delray Beach

The quintessential sports bar-restaurant-saloon with super-size satellite TV and 14 viewing screens, with a half-dozen dart boards, basketball toss and boxing ring where you don't have to get punched up, but can have a private party. The music is all 50s and 60s on the jukebox, the spirits always high, and the kitchen reliable, with a limited menu of sandwiches, burgers, pizza, beef and seafood. They're not open for breakfast but serve omelettes for those who rise late.

Shoppes of Congress Square, Congress and West Atlantic Avenues. (407) 278-7077. Inexpensive. Lunch and dinner.

SCOUNDREL'S
American/Delray Beach

The location in the basement of an office building is not exactly a plus, but the prices certainly are and so too the speedy service at lunch, the nightly entertainment, the cozy booths, omnipresence of the owners, the fresh-brewed soups and casseroles, the mouth-bending sandwiches.

100 East Linton Boulevard. (407) 265-1313. Inexpensive to moderate. Lunch, dinner and Sunday brunch.

SEACREST
American/Delray Beach

Forget the fact it's a Holiday Inn. This handsomely designed Mediterranean-Mexican-Mizner marvel stands on its own as does its penthouse restaurant. While overlooking the Atlantic, we've had excellent dinners of broiled snapper and dolphin, imaginative shrimp creations, medallions of veal in a mushroom sauce, better than average noontime buffets. The Sunday brunch is the best we've ever had in a motel.

Holiday Inn, 1229 East Atlantic Avenue. (407) 278-0882. Moderate to expensive. Lunch, dinner and Sunday brunch.

PRONTI'S ITALIAN KITCHEN
Italian/Lake Park

There has been such an incredible proliferation of Italian restaurants in recent years, spanning the gamut from the simplest mom and pop pizzeria to over-cute trattoria and grand ristorante, that we sometimes fear we will be swept away by a tidal wave of marinara sauce (clutching a Chinese red-tassel lantern of course). This place was well-established before the onslaught, opening in 1972 and steadily building a loyal corps of customers who like the from-scratch approach to the seafood and veal preparations, the homemade salad dressings, the friendliness of the staff.

1440 10th Street. (407) 842-3457. Inexpensive to moderate. Dinner.

Best Hot and Sour Soup

The flawless counterbalancing act at Feng Lin, Harbor Plaza, 1725 South Federal Highway, Delray Beach.

RAFFAELLO'S ★★
Italian/Boca Raton

In 1992 Raffaello moored a few feet closer to the ocean by moving from his former location to this Addison Mizner era home, one that's been attractively transformed into intimate dining rooms, served by a formally-clad, skilled staff. Best space for me is the Wine Room where a half dozen guests can sit in quiet comfort, surveying the cellar and deciding what to order. There are always nightly specials along with the stand-bys—Caesar salad mixed for two tableside, smoked Norwegian salmon reposing on radicchio and pastry pockets of snails with spinach and a red pepper sauce. After those good beginnings, it's time for veal scallops sauteed with capers and lemon; rack of lamb with a load of garlic plus a splash of balsamic vinaigrette and a restrained sprinkling of herbs; Dover sole or the Coniglop con Broccoli Rape, rabbit sauteed with that strong breed of Italian broccoli. The wine list is a good one albeit a bit steep in price.

725 East Palmetto Park Road. (407) 392-4855. Expensive. Dinner.

RAINBOW ROOM
American/Boca Raton

The Tremaine family, led by John and Alberta, "Bert", took over this snazzy supper club from Ciro's Pomodoro in 1993 and they've installed a new menu, one that promises "each menu selection has no more total percent of calories from fat than a stewed, skinless chicken leg." It's part of their "bodyfat management" concept and is good news when faced with such choices as pasta and Maine lobster, seafood and steaks. There's no Nautilus gear on the premises, but there is a large dance floor with lively bands, so you can burn off more calories in between bites.

1499 West Palmetto Park Road. (407) 395-9115. Expensive. Dinner.

RAINDANCER STEAK HOUSE ★★
American/West Palm Beach

Any restaurant that has survived—no, make that thrived—since 1975 in one of the most competitive markets in the world must be doing something right. Here they do everything right, from the supervision of a professional, pleasant staff to the maintenance of a non-threatening pub-club setting, from crowned-with-cheese French onion soup to the apple pie with cinnamon ice cream. In between, order the fresh fish of the day, one of the several surf and turf combinations or the beef. This is after all a steak house and their sirloins and filets are superb. So too is the privilege of having a dozen wines available by the glass from a pretty good list.

2300 Palm Beach Lakes Boulevard. (407) 684-2810. Moderate to expensive. Dinner.

THE RED LION
British/Boynton Beach

Since 1983 this strip mall pub has been South County's headquarters for bangers and mash, shepherd pies, curried chicken, Scotch eggs, and other pub grub, the kind found in hundreds if not thousands of pubs throughout the British Isles.

Plaza, 10114 South Military Trail. (407) 737-0434. Inexpensive to moderate. Dinner. No credit cards.

SIAM GARDEN
Chinese/Thai/Boca Raton

Across the street from Florida Atlantic University, this double-dragon delivers abbreviated menus of the best of two possible worlds—the bounty of the Cantonese kitchen with some Szechuan spicing mixed in, and the treats of Thai culinary tradition for those tired of the same old sweet and sour stuff. We come here for the Thai satay, the nam sod starters and anything with curry and coconut milk.

Oaks Plaza, 680 Glades Road. (407) 368-9013. Inexpensive to moderate. Lunch and dinner.

Best Vietnamese

Get your Happy Pancake and Shaking Beef at Le Truc, 297 East Palmetto Park Road, Boca Raton.

SIAM GOURMET

Thai/Boca Raton

When someone asks me in South County where to find a really good Thai restaurant or where they can be introduced to the intricacies of the special spices, curries, peppers, lemon grass and rice paper of the Land of Smiles, I invariably send them here. The food is not only superior, but owner Ead and his staff serve as the friendliest of guides. Their advice should be heeded. You won't be sorry.

23034 Sandalfoot Square. (407) 487-8414. Moderate. Lunch and dinner.

SIBERIAN RUSSIAN RESTAURANT ★★
Russian/Boca Raton

Can you believe a Siberian restaurant in lil ole Boca? One with balalaika players and Russian folk singers, with an upfront souvenir counter and a staff straight from St. Petersburg? We eat better here than we ever did there, starting with the borscht made according to the Trans-Siberian Express recipe, and the smoked dolphin, kingfish and salmon array called Kamchatka. We follow those promising beginnings with Pelmini, prepared from an original Siberian recipe and consisting of little pockets of light pastry filled with beef, chicken or vegetables and served with dill-flecked cream sauce. Of course, chicken Kiev and beef Stroganof are on the menu and they're both excellent. Ukranian beef goulash, stuffed cabbage Babuskan, chicken paprikash, and a Kremlin filet mignon round out the menu, along with a Doc Zhivago crisp-roasted duck served with grilled apple and sweet prunes. There's no Russian wine on the list—thankfully—but there is a stunning array of desserts.

2499 North Federal Highway. (407) 361-9099. Moderate to expensive. Dinner.

STILTONS
British/Boca Raton

Tucked into a third floor corner of Bloomies, just past the Petrossian Caviar Bar, is this hideaway headquarters for authentic beer-battered fish n' chips, Scottish and Irish salmon, London broil with a Buckingham brown sauce no less, Piccadilly sherried lamb, ale-battered Aussie shrimp and a variety of offerings from the Earl of Sandwich. Bass Ale on tap, Guiness and John Courage by the bottle. Blimey mates! It's the real thing.

Bloomingdales, Town Center, 5840 Glades Road. (407) 394-2265. Moderate. Lunch and dinner.

STOCKTON'S
American/Palm Beach Gardens

A few hundred yards from I-95 and a mile from the Florida Turnpike, this is a good place to break your travels with a Stockton burger smeared with smoked jalapeno lime mayo, one of the brewed-out-back superior soups, filleted in house fresh fish or the Rodeo Salad—large bowl of fresh iceberg lettuce holding up strips of honey-baked ham and chicken breast, white and jack cheese, tomato and hard boiled egg, hickory-smoked bacon.

Garden Square Shoppes, 19033 North Military Trail. (407) 775-9424. Moderate. Lunch and dinner.

SUN HAI VALLEY
Chinese/Palm Beach Gardens

Since 1985 the friendly folk in this happy valley on the corner of PGA Boulevard and Prosperity Farms Road have been building a loyal fan club which regularly lines up for the luncheon buffets and early bird specials, as well as offerings from the regular menu with Cantonese and Szechuan specialties. We like their diet dinners, featuring low calorie, low sodium, low cholesterol entrees that of course are not made with MSG.

2534 PGA Boulevard. (407) 627-9200. Inexpensive to moderate. Lunch and dinner.

Best Barbecue

The finger lickin' goodies at Tom's Place, 7251 North Federal Highway, Boca Raton.

SUNDY HOUSE
American/Delray Beach

There are many old house restaurants in South Florida, but this is the only one that also serves as antiques shop. The treasures are displayed on the two floors of a fine old home built in 1902, seven years after Flagler's iron rails reached town, by a Flagler foreman, Delray's first mayor, John Sundy. The town's first bank was born on the front porch and the First Baptist Church in the parlor. Good memories as you sit amidst the antiques or out on the porch—patio under grand old trees. The luncheon sandwiches and salads and such as rarity as Welsh Rarebit are good as are the dinners with mixed price menu and live entertainment. Among the headliners are the seafood gazpacho and bisque, center cut pork loin served with capers in a key lime sauce and fresh salmon blessed with basil butter. The sides of sweet potato and vegetable souffle are excellent.

106 Swinton Avenue. (407) 278-2163. Moderate. Lunch and dinner.

TA-BOO'
American/Palm Beach

The origins of this landmark go back to 1941 and current owners did a complete rehab in 1990. Of the several dining spaces we like the fireside room and the gazebo. For lunch we like the Caesar with grilled chicken, the fresh tuna Nicoise, smoked turkey BLT and for dinner veal paillard with watercress-cream sauce, a double New York sirloin carved tableside for two, or the lobster-luscious crabcakes.

221 Worth Avenue. (407) 835-3500. Moderate. Lunch, dinner and Sunday brunch.

TAVERN ON THE GREEN
American/Boca Raton

A spacious spread on the ground floor of one of Boca's many mod office buildings, all glass and class, with atrium tables and a comfortable banquette-filled dining room. It's a great place for the ladies who like to linger at lunch, for business meetings and romantic rendezvous-in, munching on a mesquite-grilled sirloin burger or a jumbo lump crab cake served with superb roast peppers on freshly toasted foccacia. The salads are fresh and generous in size. We like to start dinners with tuna carpaccio, carefully touched by the Japanese green fire wasabi, and then be faced with broiled dolphin mornay or salmon with a dill sauce. The piano is a nice extra touch.

Northern Trust Plaza, 301 Yamato Road. (407) 241-9214. Expensive. Lunch and dinner.

Best Continental Restaurant – Palm Beach

Cafe L'Europe is a class act all the way, 150 Worth Avenue, Palm Beach.

TESTA'S
Italian/Palm Beach

The first Palm Beach Testa set up camp in 1921 and a quarter-century later built this landmark, adding hotel, sidewalk cafe, courtyard and various family members to the management team. The menu is primarily Italian with great garlic bread and freshly-assembled pasta preparations, but be sure to save room for the strawberry pie.

221 Royal Poinciana Way. (407) 832-0992. Moderate. Breakfast, lunch and dinner.

THAI BOCA   ★★
Thai/Boca Raton

Chef Bond, veteran of the Boca Raton Hotel and Club and South Seas Plantation on Captiva wields his carving knives with the dexterity of a prize-winning sculptor. In fact, he is a sculptor—demonstrated dramatically by his deftly done carvings from tree trunks on display here. On the tables his artistry appears in the beautiful garnishes, the sliced strawberries decorating desserts and the manner in which the superior mee krob and jumping shrimp are arranged on the plate. After those promising preludes, we like to order from smiling partner Somsri the ginger pork that's sauteed with mushrooms, onions and sweet peppers and served with a fine black bean sauce; the chicken with panang curry held at bay with coconut milk; or the whole snapper zapped with red curry. Bond's desserts are also visual and gustatory pleasures. His swiftly fried bananas enclosed in pastry fluff and served with their own coconut ice cream are fantastic.

997 East Palmetto Park Road. (407) 367-0500. Inexpensive to moderate. Lunch and dinner.

THAI GOURMET
Thai/Boca Raton

It's only been a few years since the first Thai restaurant opened on the Gold Coast. Now there are well over half a hundred, including this aptly-named discovery with one of those endless menus. More than 70 items are there to please the vegetarian and all those who love the lightness and intensive flavors of traditional Thai cuisine.

Somerset Shoppes, 8309 Glades Roads. (407) 451-4145. Inexpensive to moderate. Lunch and dinner.

Best Sunday Brunch – Palm Beach

The eye-popping table groaner at The Breakers Beach Club, One South County Road, Palm Beach.

THIS IS IT PUB
American/West Palm Beach

Since the sixties, this comfy pub has built up a loyal clientele proud to proclaim This Is It, and to order such home-brewed soups as Seafood Chowder, spinach salads with bacon dressing, liverwurst and Bermuda onion sandwiches, fresh catch of the day, oyster stew, rack of lamb, penne with vodka, climaxed by grasshopper pie. The setting is nothing out of Architectural Digest, but it's the only action in this side of town.

424 24th Street. (407) 833-4997. Moderate. Lunch and dinner.

TOM JR'S RIB HEAVEN
Barbecue/Delray Beach

The son of Tom Wright, owner of Tom's Place in Boca Raton, is camped out here in this simple take-out shack with a few outdoor picnic tables. Ribs are terrific, but so too are the fried okra balls, corn on the cob, sweet potato pie—and of course the sauce. It's heavenly!

1211 South Dixie Highway. (407) 278-0505. Inexpensive. Lunch and dinner.

TOM'S PLACE
Barbecue/Boca Raton

Tom is Tom Wright, an entrepreneur who has built one of the most successful restaurants in South Florida, one that is well served by a caring crew bringing ribs and chicken with Tom's beautiful barbecue sauce, collards and corn bread. Noon or night we find it hard to resist ordering the combination platters with a lot, not a little, of everything.

7251 North Federal Highway. (407) 997-0920. Inexpensive to moderate. Lunch and dinner. No credit cards.

TOM SAWYER'S
★
American/Boca Raton

Carolina country cabin with cookie-pie-cake filled counters is the surprise inside this sleeper that is served by some of the friendliest, down-home ladies in the land. The soups are sensational, all brewed in the back and the sandwiches are real mouth-stretchers. We also like the burgers, and such blackboard specials as creamed chicken and biscuits, beef with noodles and chili—the best in the county. The huge chocolate chip cookies and the pastries are also prize-winners.

1759 Northwest Second Avenue. (407) 368-4634. Inexpensive. Breakfast and lunch.

TRATTORIA COCO LEZZONE–SICILIANA
Italian/Boca Raton

Named after a famous trattoria in Italy (does the name really mean Dirty Kitchen?), and a stage set complete with giant center table loaded with the specialties of the house, starters and finishers. Unusual pastas here are the gnocchi with a sauce made of reduced rabbit juices and perciatelli with sardines. For the main action, try the veal with non-Italian hearts of palm, mushroom and Vidalia onions. Two years after starting this indoor-outdoor cafe in 1990, the owners opened their second venture, La Trattoria in the Adirondack National Park, Old Forge, New York, as part of the local Lynn University's hotel and restaurant management program.

499 East Palmetto Park Road. (407) 393-6715. Expensive. Lunch and dinner.

TYCOONS
American/Boca Raton

A marvelously inviting oasis, opened in 1984, for Boca's up and coming tycoons—who swarm during those vital late afternoon moments known as attitude readjustment time. We come for the superbly sauteed yellowtail, the junior size snapper with a lump crabmeat fill, the garlic shrimp, prime meats, and the pleasant staff working in an eye-pleasing semi-tropical setting.

2350 Executive Center Drive. (407) 994-2269. Moderate to expensive. Dinner.

UNCLE TAI'S ★★★
Chinese/Boca Raton

Wen Dah Tai is a specialist in the intricacies of Hunan cuisine, but he also excels in the spices of Yunnan and Szechuan. Our meals start here with the diced boneless squash packages, the Szechuan dumplings or crispy quail, and move on to sliced lamb, chunked chicken, or salmon, all Szechuan style, or the pheasant, rabbit with orange, venison with garlic, duck with young ginger roots.

Crocker Center, 5250 Town Center Circle. (407) 368-8806. Expensive. Lunch and dinner.

VILLA MEDITERRANEA
Continental/Boynton Beach

Aldo Rinero is the main man here as maitre d'-manager even though Andreas Safanditis is the owner and Henry Athenosy the chef. Aldo is the veteran New York restaurateur who for years ran Palm Beach's Le Monegasque and he's putting all that experience to good use here, overseeing a marvelous space that used to be a bank which now sparkles with paintings as continental as the menu, the Eiffel Tower, Parthenon, Palm Beach's Mizner fountain and Venice. Plan your next trip as your work through a Maine lobster, duckling a l'orange, a sirloin or filet mignon.

205 Southern Boulevard. (407) 655-8455. Expensive. Lunch and dinner.

VILLA VENEZIA ★
Italian/Boca Raton

In the very definition of storefront trattoria, Little Joe and wife Liliana prepare veal and chicken 30 different ways, with judicious spicing and lots of Sicilian soul. Also noteworthy are Joe's sole Francaise, broiled red snapper, homemade ice cream and cheesecake, plus those little pizza squares—impossible to resist after ten—he uses as starters and supplements.

4135 North Federal Highway. (407) 392-5396. Moderate. Dinner. Closed mid-July to Labor Day.

VINCE
Italian/Boca Raton

After a spell away from the hassle and hectic happenings of the restaurant whirl, Vince returned to the fray in 1992, re-opening as a sometimes supper club with live entertainment. His mussels in garlic sauce are a marvelous prelude to the better than average pasta, chicken, veal and fish, prepared in the classic Italian-American manner. We usually start with those mussels and a caprese salad, followed by linguine primavera, broiled salmon, or the veal sauteed with gorgonzola and mushrooms in a scallion-showered cream sauce.

2885 South Federal Highway. (407) 278-2332. Moderate to expensive. Dinner.

VITTORIO
Italian/Delray Beach

Vittorio Mori started this comfortably elegant ristorante in 1969 as a simple snack shop with counter and stools, and now it's one of the most popular places in town. We start here with the scampi or black bean soup, move on to a small portion of tagliatelle carbonara and go for the mains of sauteed calves liver, osso buco or saltimbocca, finishing with the brandy-spiked ice cream.

25 Southeast 6th Avenue. (407) 278-5525. Expensive. Dinner. Jackets required. No credit cards.

WATERWAY CAFE
Seafood/Palm Beach

Here's the kind of Florida setting snowbirds expect to find, an outdoor-indoor class operation smack on the Intracoastal Waterway, one that is professionally run and supervised, happily staffed, and serving steamed garlic blue crabs and fried soft shells, grilled dolphin and chicken breast, fish and chips, New England scrod coated with buttered crumbs, and our favorite, the coconut-covered fried shrimp.

2300 PGA Boulevard. (407) 694-1700. Moderate. Lunch and dinner.

WATTANA THAI
Thai/West Palm Beach

Wattana is not the name of some province or exotic bird in the land of the King and I, but the name of owner Wattana Sumonthee, the talented chef in charge. We salute her success, ordering the crispy noodles and jumping shrimp or any of the sensational soups, before diving into the lobster curry with chili peppers tranquilized with coconut milk.

7201 South Dixie Highway. (407) 588-9383. Moderate. Lunch and dinner.

WILDFLOWER
American/Boca Raton

Immensely popular oasis on the waterway for the single set who rally around in the late afternoon to meet other singles and sip something stimulating at the stacked-up bar. We go for the Caesar Cobb, Chan, Dimitri and Neptune salads, the half pound pub burger, coconut battered shrimp served with raspberry or honey barbecue sauces and the bartender's steak sandwich smothered with grilled onions and provolone.

551 East Palmetto Park Road. (407) 391-0000. Moderate. Lunch and dinner.

WILT CHAMBERLAIN'S
American/Boca Raton

Yes! The one and only—Wilt the Stilt, making quite a name for himself in the sports bar—children's game—snack food department. Beware the addictive games to hook the kids— and your wallet—but do take the food seriously. Especially the Bangkok chicken-noodle salad, four cheese flat brewed pizza, turkey burger, chicken chimichanga, stir-fry primavera with Japanese soba noodles, and the barbecued beef grilled sandwich.

Somerset Shoppes, 8903 West Glades Road. (407) 488-8881. Moderate. Lunch and dinner.

ZUCKERELLO'S
Italian/Boca Raton

Palm Beach spinoffs from owner Adam Zucker's successful informal trattoria of the same name in Fort Lauderdale, these have budget-stretching luncheon buffets with a fine variety of top quality temptations. At night we like the bountiful salads, pasta freshly prepared and mingled with shrimp, chicken and broccoli, and the chicken creations. The staff is a friendly one and the supervision highly professional.

2700 North Federal Highway, (407) 394-3100; 8825 West Glades Road, (407) 483-5020. Moderate to expensive. Lunch and dinner.

Index

This index of all restaurants in the book is organized by type of cuisine. Under each cuisine listing is an alphabetical list of restaurants with their star rating (* to ****), if any, city and page number in the book.

American

Argentinean

Barbecue

Old Florida Bar-B-Que, Oakland Park, 111
Tom Jr's Rib Heaven, Delray Beach, 223
Tom's Place*, Boca Raton, 223

Brazilian

Brazilian Tropicana Restaurant, Pompano Beach, 59
Rodeo Grill, Coral Gables, 42

British

Brittania Arms, Boca Raton, 159
King's Head, The, Dania, 93
Red Lion, The, Boynton Beach, 208
Rose & Crown, The, Fort Lauderdale, 126
Stiltons, Boca Raton, 218

Cajun

Victoria Park*, Fort Lauderdale, 143

Caribbean

Mombasa Bay, Fort Lauderdale, 108

Chinese

August Moon, Hollywood, 53
Canton Garden, Boca Raton, 165
Chef Lien's, Lighthouse Point, 70
China Yung, Fort Lauderdale, 71
Chinese Fishing Village, Fort Lauderdale, 71
Crystal Palace, Coral Springs, 74
Felix Lo's*, Hollywood, 80
Feng Lin, Delray Beach, 176
Lai Lai, Boca Raton, 193
Mandarin Garden, Coconut Grove, 37
Mandarin Valley, Boca Raton, 196

Oriental Dragon, Boca Raton, 202
Pine Garden*, Boca Raton, 205
Pink Buddha, Davie, 117
Rainbow Palace***, Fort Lauderdale, 120
Royal Chef*, West Palm Beach, 211
Siam Garden, Boca Raton, 217
Silver Palace Chinese Restaurant, Deerfield Beach, 133
Sun Hai Valley, Palm Beach Gardens, 219
Uncle Tai's***, Boca Raton, 225
Wan's Mandarin House*, Fort Lauderdale, 146
Wan's Mandarin House*, Hollywood, 146

Colombian

Pancho Villa, Lake Worth, 204

Continental

A Mano**, South Miami Beach, 12
Bang**, South Miami Beach, 13
Benvenuto, Boynton Beach, 157
Biltmore, The, Coral Gables, 15
Bistro L'Europe**, Boca Raton, 158
Blue Goose Cafe**, Pembroke Pines, 57
Blue Star*, South Miami Beach, 16
Bohemian Garden, Lake Worth, 158
Boodles Grill, Dania, 58
Brickell Club, Miami, 17
Brooks****, Deerfield Beach, 60
Cafe L'Europe****, Palm Beach, 163
Cafe Tu Tu Tango, Coconut Grove, 18
Casablanca Cafe, Palm Beach, 166
Chef Reto's****, Boca Raton, 167
Christopher's, Fort Lauderdale, 72
Colony Hotel, The, Palm Beach, 168

Continental-Finnish

Cuban

Danish

Fondue

French

French-American

German

Greek

Healthfood

Hungarian

Indian

Jamaican

Japanese

Seafood